PUBLIC CAPITALISM

PUBLIC CAPITALISM

THE POLITICAL AUTHORITY
OF CORPORATE EXECUTIVES

Christopher McMahon

University of Pennsylvania Press Philadelphia

A volume in the Haney Foundation Series, established in
1961 with the generous support of Dr. John Louis Haney

Published by
University of Pennsylvania Press
Philadelphia, Pennsylvania 19104-4112
www.upenn.edu/pennpress

Printed in the United States of America on acid-free paper
10 9 8 7 6 5 4 3 2 1

Library of Congress Cataloging-in-Publication Data

McMahon, Christopher, 1945–
   Public capitalism : the political authority of corporate
executives / Christopher McMahon. — 1st ed.
      p. cm.
   Includes bibliographical references and index.
   ISBN 978-0-8122-4444-1 (alk. paper)
   1. Business ethics. 2. Executives. 3. Political ethics. 4.
Capitalism. I. Title.
HF5387.M433 2013
174′.4—dc23
                                        2012003601

*This book is dedicated to the
memory of my mother and my father
Ruth Noaks McMahon
and
George C. McMahon*

CONTENTS

INTRODUCTION

IN A MODERN capitalist society, the senior executives of large, profit-seeking corporations play an important role in shaping the collective life of the society as a whole. In this respect, they exercise social authority. Where we find social authority, we face the question of what establishes its legitimacy. This book argues that the authority exercised by corporate executives can be legitimate only if it constitutes a form of political authority. I call the species of capitalism that results *public capitalism*.

Under public capitalism, senior corporate executives, in which group I include the members of boards of directors, possess the status of public officials of a certain kind. They occupy a subordinate position in an integrated structure of cooperation-facilitating authority that is oriented toward the promotion of the public good and is under ultimate governmental control. Corporations are privately owned, but they are managed with a view to the public good. Such management is possible because profit-seeking in competitive markets, when suitably constrained, promotes one component of the public good, social prosperity.

It is customary in capitalist societies to make a distinction between the public and the private sectors. Property rights provide the basis for this distinction. The private sector of the economy uses privately owned productive resources. The public sector uses publicly owned productive resources, resources owned collectively by the members of whatever political unit is in question. The theory I present here is concerned with corporations that fall within the private sector when the public-private distinction is understood as grounded in property rights.

It might be thought, however, that economic activity in a capitalist society is private in a further sense, namely, that the normative foundation for capitalist economic activity can be provided by the morality of private life. I argue that this is not the case. As a corporation grows larger, the normative framework in which it operates changes. Actions and relations that might have been accommodated within the framework of private morality when the corporation was a small business come to require a different normative basis.

The legitimacy of social authority constitutes one of the main topics of political philosophy. Most discussion of this topic focuses on the authority of governments. It may be that the corporate case has received little attention because those governed, most notably the employees, appear to consent to government in a straightforward way. A fundamental thesis of this book, however, is that the authority exercised by corporate executives is just as problematic, from the standpoint of political philosophy, as the authority of governments and requires similarly careful investigation.

Social authority can be understood in different ways, but in its most basic form it involves a relationship marked by the issuing of directives to people who are normally prepared to comply with them. I call this form of authority *subordinating authority*.[1] In what follows, I argue that the normative apparatus of private life is not capable of establishing the legitimacy of the subordinating authority that corporate executives exercise over employees. Rather this authority must possess the same basis as the authority of legitimate governments and be exercised in concert with the authority of legitimate governments.

It is possible to understand the authority of corporate executives more broadly. Nonemployees of various kinds—for example, investors, creditors, or suppliers—contribute in different ways to the activities of a corporation, and the senior executives determine the form these contributions will ultimately take, the way they will find expression in corporate actions. To the extent that nonemployee contributors can be regarded as deferring to the judgment of corporate executives concerning the way their contributions will find expression in corporate actions, there is a sense in which corporate executives exercise authority over these people as well. Moreover, in exercising this authority over nonemployee contributors, executives can be viewed as performing a public function. The theory of public capitalism encompasses this broader role as well, but the argument that corporate executives must be understood as exercising a kind of political authority takes as its point of departure the legitimacy of the subordinating authority that executives exercise over employees.

The main argument has several steps and is spread over Chapters 2 and 3, but the basic idea can be stated here. Governments issue directives, laws and regulations, that are intended to give political cooperation a certain shape. They also support these directives with coercive sanctions. Penalties are imposed on those who fail to obey the law. This gives governments what I call *directive power*. But we do not regard the fact that a government possesses directive power as sufficient to establish its legitimacy. Totalitarian governments possess directive power. Legitimacy requires that there be sufficient reason, independent of the directive power the government exercises over the members of a polity, for the members to comply with the government's directives. I suggest a candidate for this reason in Chapter 3.

3

The argument concerning corporate executives is that the situation we find in large, profit-seeking corporations is analogous to the governmental situation. Corporate executives issue directives intended to give corporate cooperation a certain shape. Compliance with these directives is supported by the threat of a penalty for noncompliance, the termination of employment. Corporate executives thus possess directive power with respect to a corporation's employees, the ultimate basis of which is provided by corporate property rights. But directive power is not legitimate authority. Therefore, if we are to understand corporate executives as exercising legitimate subordinating authority over employees, we need to establish that there is sufficient reason, independent of the directive power to which employees are subject, for them to comply with the directives they receive.

I argue that this reason must be of the same kind as, and integrated with, the reason that establishes the legitimacy of government. To be legitimate, the authority exercised by corporate executives must constitute a subordinate form of political—that is, public—authority. Because legitimate authority is normatively prior to directive power, constraining the exercise of that power, corporate property rights, as defined by the law, must take a form that is compatible with these results concerning legitimacy.

I also explore a second reason that the actions of corporate executives must be placed within the normative framework of public decision making. The performance of their official duties sometimes requires public officials to treat citizens in ways that private persons are not normally permitted to treat one another. Such actions are justified by the belief that they are necessary if the public good is to be effectively promoted. Thus the defense of a country may require some deception of its citizens. I argue that certain actions performed by corporate executives require an analogous justification if they are to be understood as morally permissible. The principal example is inflicting the harm that often accompanies the laying off of employees or the closing of plants in communities that depend on them. In many cases, these actions cannot be justified merely because they serve the interests of the owners or investors. Actions of this kind can also be performed by the managers of small businesses, but these actions are more socially consequential when performed by the executives of large corporations.

In Chapter 1, I explain the distinction between the public and the private. I then turn to the argument that the authority exercised by the senior executives of large, profit-seeking corporations must be understood as a kind of political authority. In Chapter 2, I argue that the moral framework of private life is not capable of establishing the legitimacy of the subordinating authority exercised by the executives of large, profit-seeking corporations. In Chapter 3, I show how understanding this authority as a kind of political authority solves the problems encountered by the private model. In Chapter 4, I explore the possibility that the official duties of corporate executives can involve treating individuals in a manner that would ordinarily be morally impermissible. Finally, in Chapter 5, I trace some consequences for managerial decision making of the idea that corporate executives exercise a form of political authority.

My argument uses (what I take to be) the fact that questions of political morality admit of reasonable disagreement. I explore this idea in *Reasonable Disagreement: A Theory of Political Morality*.[2] Political decision making typically resolves reasonable moral disagreement within the political unit in question. The theory of public capitalism that I present here views the executives of large corporations as making political decisions of this sort. The theory views them as resolving reasonable moral disagreement, among the members of their corporations, and also within the larger society, about the appropriate way to structure the parts of the overall system of political cooperation that are under their control. This is another respect in which they perform a public function.

It should be emphasized that this book is a work of political philosophy. It uses the concepts and methods of political philosophy to construct an argument that the senior executives of large, profit-seeking corporations should be understood as exercising a form of political authority. This is not the only way to approach authority relations within corporations. A well-developed literature in economics studies how different governance structures affect economic efficiency. As formulated by Oliver Williamson, this approach is based on the idea that if we take people as they are, with their various limitations, ordinary market contracting cannot by itself achieve efficient outcomes, and consequently hierarchical governance structures are required. Such governance structures promote efficiency by economizing on transaction costs. Williamson characterizes this project as follows: "[T]ransaction cost economics maintains the rebuttable presumption that organizational variety arises primarily in the service of transaction cost economizing. That approach is to be distinguished not merely from the technological approach to economic organization but also from power approaches, which ascribe nonstandard forms of organization to monopoly purposes or class interests."[3]

Corporate governance is also studied from a more general perspective by writers who investigate how corporations should be governed to ensure that legitimate corporate goals are achieved, where these goals are typically understood in terms of the interests of investors or a larger group of "stakeholders." A central topic in this literature is the difficulty of controlling agents who possess more knowledge than the people on whose behalf they are acting.

Stephen Bainbridge's *The New Corporate Governance in Theory and Practice* is an informative example of this approach.[4] Focusing on the United States, where, he says, there is a legal consensus that publicly held corporations should be managed in the interest of the shareholders, Bainbridge considers who does, and who should, actually control such corporations. He advocates a view he calls "board primacy," according to which effective control should be, and increasingly is, exercised by the board of directors. This view presupposes a picture of the corporation as a nexus of explicit and implicit contracts in which the board of directors functions as the central contractor. Bainbridge thus rejects both the view that shareholders do, or should, exercise ultimate control and the view known as managerialism, which locates ultimate control in the chief executive officer and the people immediately subordinate to him or her.

It is not my intention to offer a replacement for these well-developed research programs. I believe, though, that exploring the role played by corporate executives from the standpoint of political philosophy enables us to gain insight into the place of economic activity in a modern capitalist society that is not obtainable in any other way. Williamson and Bainbridge both understand corporate governance in terms of economic efficiency. For public capitalism, however, the criterion for successful corporate governance is promotion of the public good. Economic efficiency is closely associated with a particular moral value, the value of social prosperity, which is an important component of the public good. But other components are important as well. Defenders of alternative approaches to corporate governance may reply that the promotion of the public good is a task for political, in contrast to corporate, decision making. For public capitalism, however, corporate decision making is a species of political decision making.

My argument in this book applies to all societies containing large, privately owned, profit-seeking corporations. The implications are doubtless most radical in countries like the United

States, where corporate decision making is focused on serving the interests of shareholders and other investors. Elsewhere, corporate executives may confront a legal framework, or informal social pressures, that force them to accommodate the interests of additional stakeholders, especially employees, more fully than is the case in the United States. In those countries, the idea that corporate executives exercise a form of political authority might have greater intuitive plausibility. Nevertheless, an argument is required to establish that they do, in fact, exercise such authority.

It may be helpful, finally, to expand a little on what is accomplished by approaching the issues discussed in this book from the standpoint of political philosophy. As mentioned earlier, discussions of corporate governance in management studies typically emphasize economic efficiency. Thus John Boatright ties the governance structures characteristic of profit-seeking corporations to efficient investment.[5]

The theory of public capitalism presented in this book is not concerned with corporate governance in the sense of the management studies literature. It is concerned with the social authority that corporate executives possess within the societies where their corporations are located. I term this *managerial authority*. The theory of public capitalism is a theory of the legitimacy of managerial authority. As is customary in political philosophy, the argument is addressed not to a particular group within the larger society but to the society as a whole. It aims to provide a way for all of us living in modern capitalist societies to think about the role that corporate decision making plays in our lives, a way that views this decision making from the standpoint of our purposes as a group of people—a society—cooperating politically to promote the public good.

1

THE PUBLIC AND THE PRIVATE

THE IDEA THAT the managers of the major productive enterprises operating within a society should be understood as exercising a kind of political authority seems at first sight to require socialism. In socialist systems, most productive enterprises are owned by the state and their managers are functionaries of the state. Historically, the main attempts to establish socialist systems have involved the replacement of the market, as the social device that determines what will be produced, by a central plan. But market socialism, in which publicly owned enterprises produce for the market, is also a possibility. Market socialism seeks to preserve in a market context the socialist ideal of an economy run for the benefit of the workers. Such a system was found in the former Yugoslavia.

In our contemporary world, however, the operation of publicly owned productive enterprises in competitive markets is more likely to take the form of what is coming to be called "state capitalism." Here, the goal of the arrangement is not, directly at least, to benefit workers but to provide revenue for, or otherwise serve the purposes of, a country's government. Often the government is authoritarian or in some other way not under full democratic control. The phenomenon is most visible in the energy sector, where state-owned energy companies are dominant.[1]

In this book, I focus on polities that have opted for a standard capitalist system, understood as one in which most productive property is privately owned and most productive enterprises are responsible for their own financial viability.[2] Henceforth, when I speak of a capitalist system, I shall have such a system in mind. The main thrust of this book's argument is that even when a polity possesses a standard capitalist system, the senior executives of its large corporations should be understood as exercising a form of political authority. Once this becomes clear, the choice between capitalism and socialism, which has played a central role in the history of the modern world and continues to be treated as a live issue in many countries, may seem to possess less moral significance.

In this chapter, I set the stage for the main argument by exploring in a general way the distinction between the public and the private.

The Private Sector

As noted in the Introduction, it is customary to distinguish two sectors of a capitalist economy: the public and the private. I understand the privacy of the corporations in the private sector to be a matter of legal ownership. Private ownership, as I am going to interpret it, is defined in negative terms. A corporation is privately owned when it is not owned by the state, where this includes ownership by departments or agencies of the state. Standard accounts of legal ownership resolve it into a number of different rights. The most important are the right to exclude others from an item, the right to use the item, the right to manage the item's use by others, the right to the income derived from putting the item to productive use, and the right to sell or otherwise alienate the item.[3] A corporation is owned by the state, I shall suppose, when the state or one of its agencies possesses all or most of these rights with respect to that corporation. A corporation is thus privately owned if all or most of these rights are held by private individuals or by legal entities that are not agencies of the state. The legal owners of a private corporation can be understood to comprise all of the people or entities to whom any of the incidents of ownership have been legally assigned.

In the United States, some profit-seeking corporations that are private in the sense just described are said to be publicly held, meaning that important incidents of ownership are assigned to a set of shareholders who can sell their shares in established markets. A publicly held corporation is legally required to make a report of its financial condition to the public and thus to actual or potential shareholders. A privately held corporation does not issue publicly traded shares and does not face such a legal requirement. The "public" that holds the shares of a publicly held corporation will usually include private individuals and entities such as pension funds or institutional endowments.

When I speak of large, profit-seeking corporations, I primarily have in mind large, publicly held corporations. Corporations of this kind form the core of a modern capitalist economy. But my argument that the senior executives of capitalist corporations should be understood as exercising a kind of political authority also applies to privately held corporations if they are large enough. As I explain in Chapter 2, the authority possessed by corporate executives cannot be grounded in property rights. Differences in the ownership structures found in a modern capitalist economy thus have no bearing on the political status of corporate executives.

Some corporations in the United States do not seek profits, however, and something should be said about these. One group consists of not-for-profit mutual-benefit corporations—Chambers of Commerce, for example—which are typically financed by member contributions that are not tax deductible. Another group consists of not-for-profit public-benefit corporations. Contributions to corporations of this kind are usually tax deductible. In some cases, contributors can acquire the status of members, and the boards of directors of a public-benefit corporation may be selected by its members. Examples of not-for-profit public-benefit corporations include certain public radio and television stations.[4]

A corporation is a legal entity of a particular kind, formed when one or more people incorporate. In the case of not-for-profit public-benefit corporations, the larger society makes incorporation available as a way to serve public purposes. There is controversy, however, about what possessing the legal status of a corporation implies in the case of profit-seeking corporations. Is a profit-seeking corporation merely a legal instrument by which certain people can advance their private interests? Or is corporate status conferred by the state with the expectation that corporations of this kind, too, will serve some public purposes?[5]

The argument I present in this book is a normative political argument, an argument concerning how political cooperation ought to be organized. It is thus independent of statutory and case law. I argue that the social authority held by corporate executives is legitimate only if it constitutes a form of political authority. Legitimacy derives from the fact that the corporations are managed as subordinate centers of cooperation in a larger cooperative structure, under ultimate governmental control, that is oriented toward the promotion of the public good.

The argument has implications for corporate law, however. Just as the legal system as a whole must take a form that is consistent with the legitimacy of government, so corporate law must take a form that is consistent with the legitimacy of the authority exercised by corporate executives. Under public capitalism, corporate decision making must be guided, ultimately, by a competently reasoned conception of the public good. So the legal system will have to provide for such guidance, either through the legal regulation of corporate activities or through the establishment of a body of corporate law that gives executives the flexibility to act on competently reasoned conceptions of the public good.

13

The implications for corporate property rights deserve special notice. My argument assumes that there are no natural property rights in productive resources. People may, simply by the nature of things, have property in their persons. They may own themselves. But their rights with respect to productive property are socially defined and, in the most important cases, legally defined. The decisions that establish the different rights associated with ownership of productive resources, and that assign these rights to particular people or legal entities, are made by the larger society with a view to the public good.

The supposition that there are natural property rights in productive resources—that ownership has a moral basis that would still exist in a pre-political condition where there were no laws—is a feature of John Locke's political theory.[6] There, the principal resource in question is land. For Locke, ownership of an un-owned item is acquired by "mixing one's labor" with it, provided there is "as much and as good" left for others. Thus one acquires property rights in a fish in the ocean by hooking it. Similarly, un-owned land can be appropriated by developing it. The owner of productive resources also owns what these resources produce. Presumably, this includes productive resources of other kinds. Thus a landowner might use some of what his land produces to build a factory.

This picture is of doubtful relevance today, however. In the modern world, almost all property that is legitimately acquired is acquired by voluntary transfer from prior owners. For an example of Lockean original appropriation, we need to look to something like the assembling of a bug collection. Within the Lockean framework, it must be possible to trace the ownership of something acquired by voluntary transfer through a series of prior voluntary transfers to permissible acts of original appropriation. Robert Nozick suggests that the Lockean proviso concerning "as much and as good" can be interpreted as a requirement that appropriation not worsen the situation of nonowners, and he notes that this constraint applies to subsequent transfers.[7] They, too, must not worsen the situation of nonowners, relative to an initial situation where there is no private property. Nozick argues that current property arrangements can be understood as meeting this condition. The institution of private property in productive resources has given nonowners a higher standard of living than they would have had in the absence of that institution.

Even if this is true, however, it does not follow that the current possessors of productive property are legitimate owners. It is obvious that the history of private property has not been a history of voluntary transfers originating in permissible acts of original appropriation. Rather, to a significant extent, de facto possession brought about in a variety of ways, including force and fraud, has been ratified by the law. Nozick's entitlement theory of justice in holdings provides for the rectification of wrongful transfers, but it is unclear what this would entail in our current circumstances. As a result, the acceptability, as a matter of Lockean natural right, of the present pattern of ownership of productive resources is open to question.

We must, then, look to the law to provide a normative basis for ownership of productive resources in the modern world. This supports the "concession" view of incorporation, according to which corporate status is granted by the state as a means of promoting the public good. The opposing "inherence" view holds that the right to incorporate inheres in private ownership of productive resources and thus that owners do not need the imprimatur of the state to form a corporation. But even if a corporation is understood simply as a nexus of contracts, it is still a legal entity. The associated rights, obligations, powers, and immunities are defined by the law. Property owners in a Lockean state of nature have a natural right to form joint ventures with other owners. But they cannot form corporations because a corporation is a legal entity, and there is no government, and thus no law, in a Lockean state of nature. Incorporation presupposes the state. The inherence theory is a particular view about how the state makes, or ought to make, incorporation available to the legal owners of productive resources. It ought to make incorporation available at the discretion of the owners. The right to incorporate to achieve private purposes is thus conceded by the state in the expectation that giving people this right will be conducive to the public good.

The implications for public capitalism are straightforward. Public capitalism is a theory of the legitimacy of the authority exercised by corporate executives. It specifies that this authority is legitimately exercised only if it has the status of a subordinate form of authority within a larger structure under ultimate governmental control. Public capitalism thus places limits on the way corporate executives can use productive property. But there can be no argument that these limits are unacceptable because they conflict with the property rights of the corporation's owners. The rights associated with incorporation are defined by the law, and corporate law can be given whatever form is necessary to ensure that the authority exercised by corporate executives is legitimate. Legitimacy requires that executives act on a competently reasoned conception of the public good, but as I explain in Chapters 3 and 5, this can be compatible with profit-seeking in a competitive environment.

Public and Private Morality

A framework of moral requirements governs interaction among individuals. Let's call this *private morality.* Some of the requirements are captured by familiar, commonsense moral principles, such as those that prescribe refraining from assault, keeping promises, helping people in distress, and respecting other people's personal property. These requirements can be provided with a foundation in different ways, but one possibility is that the actions mentioned are necessary to honor claims to fair treatment. If this is right, the familiar principles can be regarded as identifying particular kinds of fair or unfair treatment that have, in the course of human history, acquired salience. It is unfair to advance one's ends by assaulting people or by breaking promises.

The requirements governing interaction among individuals create for each individual a space within which she can give her life a distinctive shape determined by her particular concerns. To put it differently, the requirements governing interaction among individuals correspond to ways we must treat people if we are to respect their status as authors of distinctive human lives, lives marked by commitments and pursuits that need not be shared by other people. In this way, the requirements enable each individual to conduct a private life.

Individuals functioning in a public capacity, by contrast, are oriented toward the good of the society as a whole. The good of a society can be resolved into a number of component goods possessing moral significance. On the way of understanding these goods that I favor, they include forms of aggregate well-being within a human population. I call these *morally important social values.* One such value is distributive justice, which many writers understand to require that disparities of wealth and income not exceed a certain level. Maintaining a satisfactory pattern of distribution within a society can be understood as required by the value of fairness applied on a social scale.[8]

Other morally important social values are grounded in considerations of human welfare. A partial list of such welfare-based values would include social prosperity, the preservation of the environment (to the extent that it affects human welfare), the fostering of community, the maintenance of the health of the population, the advancement of knowledge (understood broadly as encompassing the creation of an educated and informed populace), and the development of culture. National defense and the rule of law are further morally important social values, although they may be grounded in more than welfare. The appropriate reconciliation of all the moral considerations that govern the actions of individuals functioning in a public capacity, the requirements of private morality and the morally important social values, can be termed the *public good*. An understanding of how these different considerations ought to be balanced against one another will thus constitute a conception of the public good.

The value of distributive justice can be seen as a kind of public-private hybrid. Justice is a social value—John Rawls calls justice the first virtue of social institutions—but it plays a role in protecting the ability of the members of a polity to lead distinctive lives.[9] One way it does this is by governing the distribution, within the polity, of the means of life.[10] We can imagine cases where the value of justice conflicts with other morally important social values; for example, when an artistic genius demands exorbitant compensation for giving the society the products of her genius. Here distributive justice conflicts with the development of culture. More commonly, however, justice and the other morally important social values will be co-realizable. The welfare-based values correspond to forms of aggregate well-being in a human population, but they can also present issues of distribution. Thus maintaining the health of the population is a morally important social value, but it is accomplished in the first instance by distributing health care to individuals. So we can ask whether the distribution is just. When justice overlaps in this way with a morally important social value, justice grounds rights to receive goods or services that contribute to realization of the value.

An individual can function in a public capacity, a way that is guided by a conception of the public good, without being a public official. We typically speak of such people as performing a public service. Thus someone who reports a brush fire that, if not extinguished, would threaten a town, performs a public service, even if he is not a public official. To take another example, in describing newspapers in nineteenth-century France, a recent article says, "[I]t becomes obvious how efficiently the literary depiction of daily life functioned as a public service."[11] In cases of this sort, the promotion of the public good takes place within the framework of private morality. It does not involve any violation of the requirements of private morality, and the agent is not required to sacrifice the pursuits that are distinctive of his life. Indeed, as the example concerning the literary depiction of daily life shows, the performance of a public service can be among the pursuits that make up a distinctive human life.

But the public good has a consequentialist aspect, and there is a danger that an agent who is fully responsive to the demands of consequentialist moral considerations will not be able to live a life in which distinctive pursuits, that have meaning for him but need not have meaning for anyone else, occupy a central place. In general, there is always more that a given individual can do to promote a particular consequentialist goal. The point is often made in connection with a utilitarian requirement to act in every situation so as to maximize human welfare, construed simply as total aggregate want-satisfaction. Most people in the wealthier parts of the world could make a bigger contribution to human welfare than they are now making by donating all the money they spend on such things as vacations, restaurant meals, and theater tickets to charities that help the poor. The gains to the recipients would more than compensate for the loss to the donors. And the logic of welfare maximization dictates doing this until one's standard of living has been reduced to that of the people most in need of help.

It is widely accepted, however, that a personal sacrifice this extreme, while perhaps commendable, is not morally required. Thus some contemporary moral theorists have suggested that individual agents enjoy a permission or prerogative to decline to sacrifice their central commitments and pursuits simply because this would have morally good consequences.[12] The point applies to the morally important social values I have identified. By increasing one's charitable contributions, one could doubtless act more effectively to promote public health in the country where one resides or to foster the development of its culture, and there is no upper limit on the financial sacrifices that these values can justify. The point holds as well for nonfinancial contributions to the promotion of such values—for example, donations of labor. Such nonfinancial contributions may be among the pursuits that give an individual's life a distinctive character. But this will not be true for everyone.

People acting in a private capacity are not, then, required to make sacrifices that would force them to surrender their status as authors of distinctive lives organized around particular commitments and pursuits. As we shall see, however, the morally important social values can sometimes justify public officials, whose positions make them responsible for promoting the public good, in imposing on private individuals sacrifices that can threaten their distinctive commitments and pursuits. Both of these points—the freedom of individuals to decline to sacrifice the pursuits that give their lives a distinctive shape and the permissibility of the imposition of such sacrifices by public officials—will play a role in the arguments that follow.

19

This way of characterizing the public-private distinction turns on a difference in the normative frameworks within which people functioning in these two capacities operate. The requirements of private morality, taken together, give individual agents a reason to conduct themselves in a way that respects the status of other individuals as authors of distinctive lives. The framework guiding people acting in a public capacity, which we can call *public morality*, combines the requirements of private morality with a set of morally important social values. A view of what is required by all these considerations taken together is a conception of the public good.

Because public morality includes the requirements of private morality, agents guided by public morality must take into account the effects their actions will have on the status of individuals as authors of distinctive human lives. But public morality does not give agents operating within its framework the discretion to decline its demands because complying with them would require too great a sacrifice. To the extent that agents have this discretion, it is because they have a permission or prerogative, provided by private morality, to remove themselves from the framework of public morality when they deem this necessary to preserve their status as authors of distinctive lives. Thus a public official who finds that discharging her official duties conflicts with her distinctive commitments and pursuits is not required to sacrifice them, but she is required to resign if she wishes to indulge them.

Public Officials

As was mentioned in the Introduction, if the authority exercised by the senior executives of profit-seeking corporations constitutes a form of political authority, these people will have the status of public officials. We can obtain an understanding of what is involved in being a public official by combining the account of the public-private distinction just presented with an account of what it is to function as an official. The words *official* and *office* are used in a variety of ways. As I am going to use them, they presuppose the concept of a collective agent. A collective agent consists of a group of people, the agent's members, acting in a coordinated way to achieve common goals. Particular individuals can be authorized to perform specific actions on behalf of a collective agent. When an individual is authorized to act on behalf of a collective agent, he or she is acting in an official capacity.

One can act in an official capacity without being an official. A large corporation is a collective agent in the sense just described, and arguably, any employee of a corporation is acting in an official capacity when he performs the tasks he has been assigned. Thus a mechanic changing an oil filter on a company vehicle could be said to be acting in an official capacity. An official, by contrast, is an individual who not only acts on behalf of a collective agent but whose tasks involve interacting with other people, either members of the collective agent or outsiders, in ways that require an exercise of judgment concerning what would further the goals of the collective agent.

The definition may seem too broad. It could be satisfied by any employee of a corporation who represents it in its dealings with the public—for example, a service technician for a cable company. We can address this problem by introducing a sliding scale of "officiality." A service technician's decisions concerning whether the goals of the cable company are being met will play a relatively minor role in the achievement of those goals, so she will be an official in only a minor sense. For present purposes, it will be enough if the definition covers all the people who would, intuitively, be regarded as officials of a collective agent.

An official need not be a member of the collective agent on whose behalf she acts. She might simply be someone who has

21

undertaken to perform a task, or set of tasks, that requires the requisite exercise of judgment. An ambassador could have this status. However, most officials of a collective agent will be members. Of officials who are members, the most important are those who exercise subordinating authority over other members. Officials of this kind determine what the collective agent will do, what collective actions it will perform. Subordinating authority plays no role in the actions of some collective agents. A number of people who join together to right an overturned car will constitute a collective agent, but there will be no authority relations. Subordinating authority enters the picture when a collective agent is expected to remain in existence for some time and respond in an appropriate way to changing circumstances—that is, to adjust its actions so as to continue to achieve its goals in new circumstances.

The exercise of subordinating authority over the members of a collective agent presupposes the existence of a decision procedure, a mechanism by which the agent can decide what to do. Possible procedures include voting and the exercise of some kind of dictatorship. But the decisions produced will be pointless unless the members can be expected to put them into effect. This is typically accomplished through the issuing of directives that specify how each member is to contribute to the collective effort.

The distinctive mark of subordinating authority exercised over the members of a collective agent is that the members are prepared to defer to the relevant directives, where deferring means doing what they are directed to do even when they judge that some other course of action would be best in the circumstances. Authority of this sort can be understood as a kind of social fact, an ability to get the members of a collective agent to do certain things simply by directing them to do these things. We can speak in this connection of *de facto authority*. Ordinarily, however, the threat of a penalty of some sort for noncompliance will also play a role. The general ability of a source of directives within a collective agent to secure compliance from the members—simply by issuing the directives or because there will be a penalty for noncompliance—may or may not be supported by a separate justification for compliance. When it has this support, we can speak of *legitimate authority*.[13] Where authority is legitimate, those over whom it is exercised have sufficient reason to comply with the directives they receive, regardless of whether they will incur a penalty for noncompliance. These points are discussed in more detail in Chapters 2 and 3.

I have suggested that the most important officials of a collective agent are those who, because they possess subordinating authority within the group of people constituting the agent, are able to guide its endeavors. On this way of understanding official action, there need be no public activity involved. Private individuals sharing a pursuit that is protected from encroachment by consequentialist moral considerations might join together to form a collective agent—for example, a tennis club.

We can provide an account of what is involved in being a public official by adding to the observations just made our earlier discussion of the public-private distinction. The simplest case concerns officials of the state. The state can be regarded as a collective agent comprising all the residents of a particular territory. To view the residents as constituting a collective agent is to understand them as coordinating their actions to achieve some common goals. This is discussed further in Chapter 3, but broadly speaking, the members of a state cooperate to promote the public good, as described earlier. That is, they cooperate to implement a conception of the public good—a reasonable conception, it is hoped—generated by the political decision-making process. It is because political cooperation has the goal of promoting the public good that the officials of the state are public officials. Of the officials of the state, the most important are those who exercise subordinating authority over the members of the state. Their directives facilitate cooperation within the state to promote the public good. Collectively, they constitute the government of the state.

Governmental officials make moral judgments concerning how political cooperation ought to be organized. These moral judgments, taken together, constitute the conception of the public good guiding political cooperation within the state. Making these judgments involves deciding how to reconcile the claims of the various morally important social values. But it also involves deciding how to resolve conflicts between the morally important social values and the requirements of private morality. Governmental officials may decide that certain efforts to promote the morally important social values would unacceptably compromise the status of various members of the state as authors of distinctive lives. Conversely, they may decide that respecting this status would require too great a sacrifice of various morally important social values.

A clear example is provided by military conscription. The decision to implement conscription can be understood as grounded in a judgment that respecting the status of members of the state as authors of distinctive lives would involve too great a sacrifice of the morally important social value of national defense. The decision to establish an all-volunteer military, by contrast, can be understood as grounded in a judgment that conscription would unacceptably compromise the status of members of the state as authors of distinctive lives.

A typical modern state—that is, a nation—will contain a number of smaller collective agents. Examples include clubs, churches, trade unions, and professional associations. All of these collective agents are subject to the authority of the government in the sense that they must obey the law. But to the extent that they seek to promote private purposes, their officials are not public officials. A modern state, or nation, will also, however, contain smaller centers of collective action that are actually part of the governing apparatus of the state. Governmental departments or agencies are examples of such centers. In a federal system, component states (as in "the several states of the United States") or provinces constitute another example, as do municipalities.

The people who exercise authority within governmental departments or agencies are public officials because the departments or agencies they supervise have the institutional role of putting into effect laws enacted by legislators seeking to promote the public good. Officials of lower-level governments in a federal system are public officials in the first instance by virtue of the fact that the concept of the public good finds application in connection with component states and municipalities. That is, we can speak of the public good of a component state or municipality. There is also a sense, however, in which officials in these lower-level governments function as public officials within the nation as a whole.

The cooperation that takes place within a component state or municipality forms a part of the larger cooperative effort to promote the public good at the national level. The good of the nation is affected by what goes on in the states and municipalities it contains, and the national government may enact laws and regulations designed to give the cooperation taking place at the state and municipal levels a shape that will enable it to contribute to the public good of the nation as a whole. For example, the national government may mandate certain educational policies. To the extent that this is so, the governments of these political units play a subordinate cooperation-facilitating role within a larger cooperative effort guided by the national government. Subordinate governments may also take considerations related to the good of the nation as a whole into account in making policy decisions that are not legally mandated by the national government. Thus environmental legislation might be enacted at the state level in part because the state, or its government, thinks that this would benefit the nation as a whole. In this respect as well, state officials will be playing a cooperation-facilitating role in the larger entity.

This brings us, at last, to large, profit-seeking corporations. They, too, are collective agents contained within the state, or nation. Moreover, the decisions made within large corporations have a substantial impact on the realization of the public good at the national level. I am going to argue that this fact has consequences for the legitimacy of the subordinating authority exercised by the executives of a large corporation. The executives of a large corporation can claim legitimate authority over the members of the corporation only if the activities they supervise constitute component parts of a larger cooperative enterprise, under the ultimate control of the national government, aimed at the promotion of the public good in the nation as a whole. That is, managerial authority in a large corporation can be regarded as legitimately exercised only if it is understood as a subordinate form of cooperation-facilitating authority in a larger structure of such authority, the overall purpose of which is to guide the nation as a whole to the realization of the public good.[14]

It follows that when the executives of a large corporation are exercising legitimate authority, they are functioning as subordinate public officials. They are acting on behalf of the polity as a whole. This is true, moreover, even if the corporation began life as a small business, the operation of which was a protected private pursuit. As a small business grows into a large corporation, its founder acquires the status of a public official.

This claim deserves emphasis. It is not just that corporate executives, by organizing the provision of goods and services and by providing employment, perform a public service. Arguably anyone operating a legal business performs a public service in this sense. The claim is that, by virtue of the conditions under which corporate executives can be regarded as exercising legitimate authority—and also, as will be discussed in Chapter 4, by virtue of certain of the actions they are justified in taking in this capacity—they have the status, within the larger political society, of subordinate public officials. They play a role in the larger social effort to promote the public good analogous to that played by the heads of governmental departments and agencies or by the leaders of the governments of subordinate political units such as states or municipalities.

The Moral Status of Corporations

Corporations are legal persons, artificial persons of a particular sort. As such, they possess legal rights and obligations. It might be thought that corporations can also be understood as moral persons—that the set of moral persons should be understood as containing not only human beings but also corporations. This would mean that corporations have moral rights, duties, and obligations.[15] The issue here is of some importance. Ideally, the legal rights and obligations of a moral person will reflect, in important respects, his, her, or its moral rights and obligations. For example, because moral persons have a right to express their political opinions, in a well-designed polity they will have a corresponding legal right. It follows that if corporations are moral persons, they, too, should have this legal right. But if corporations are not moral persons, if their personhood is simply a legal fiction, their rights and obligations must be approached differently, via the question of what assignment of rights and obligations would have the best consequences for the public good as a whole. In this concluding section, I argue that although corporations are legal persons, they cannot coherently be understood as moral persons.

Understanding corporations as moral persons will be pointless unless what morality requires or permits a corporation to do can diverge from what morality requires or permits the associated human beings, the corporation's members, acting collectively, to do. Suppose there is such a divergence. How would the conflict be resolved? A corporation is a whole that has individual human beings as parts. One possibility, therefore, is that what it is required or permitted to do takes precedence over what its members, considered as human beings, are required or permitted to do. If it faces an imperative to grow in strength and internal articulation—if it has such a "duty to itself"—the associated individuals must accommodate this imperative despite the fact that there is no duty at the human level to perform the corresponding actions. As a concrete example, we might take the forced industrialization in the Soviet Union during the Stalinist period. One way of interpreting what took place is that the leaders of the Soviet Union regarded themselves as the servants of a social entity, the state, whose needs as an organism of a certain kind took precedence over the requirements governing interaction among human beings.

A little reflection, however, shows that any conflict between moral requirements or permissions that apply to corporations and the moral requirements or permissions that apply to human beings must actually be resolved in favor of the latter. What a corporation does supervenes on the actions, or more broadly the behavior, of its members. The concept of supervenience marks a way that lower-level facts determine upper-level facts. Thus the beauty of a piece of music supervenes on its properties as a sequence of sounds, properties that could be described by a physicist. In the corporate case, the lower-level facts are facts about human beings and the upper-level facts are facts about the corporation. So the supervenience of what a corporation does on what its members do means that the actions or behavior of the members determine what the corporation does.

As a consequence, there can be no basis for adding to our moral theory requirements or permissions that apply to corporations if what is required or permitted can depart from what the associated human beings, acting collectively, are required or permitted to do. What a corporation does will be determined by what its members do, and they are appropriately guided by the moral considerations that apply to them as human beings, not by moral considerations that apply to entities of a different kind. Thus the only moral considerations that can actually play a role in shaping the behavior of a corporation will be those that apply to the human beings who are its members. What the members are required or permitted to do establishes the moral framework within which the actions of the corporation, as a moral agent, must unfold. But then giving corporations the status of moral persons will be empty of practical significance. It either will involve the introduction of requirements and permissions that can have no practical effect because they conflict with what the members as human beings are required or permitted to do or will be redundant because what is required or permitted at the corporate level is something the members are already required or permitted to do.

Regarding a corporation as a moral person operating within its own space of moral reasons would be possible if the human beings constituting its members played the same role in its practical life that the muscles of a human being play in her practical life. What she has sufficient reason to do determines what her muscles, insofar as their movements are guided by reason, will do. Similarly, what the corporation had sufficient reason to do would determine what its members, insofar as their movements were guided by reason, would do. But the human beings who are the members of a corporation do not have the same status as the muscles of a human body. They are rational beings in their own right, living in their own space of reasons. And because what they do determines what the corporation does, what they have reason to do will determine what the corporation does, insofar as its actions are guided by reason. There is, then, no place in a coherent moral theory for the idea that corporations are moral persons.

One implication of this result deserves special mention. Because corporations are not moral persons, they do not have the prerogative or permission that protects the status of human beings as authors of distinctive lives. This means that when charting a moral course for their corporation, senior executives cannot exercise such a prerogative on the corporation's behalf.

A more general lesson can also be drawn from these observations. There is no place in a coherent theory of rational agency for two levels of rational guidance, one applying to wholes of a certain kind and the other to their parts. Given the supervenience of the actions of the whole on the actions of the parts, the level of rational guidance that governs the actions of the parts will also govern the actions of the whole. We can make a place in *human* life for collective agents, and these have other agents as parts. But no second level of rational guidance is involved. The existence of a collective agent rather reflects the fact that human beings whose cognitive and motivational capacities are functioning properly will be prepared, under certain circumstances, to coordinate their actions so as to achieve common goals. Any rights and obligations possessed by a collective agent must thus be derived from the rights and obligations of the human beings who are its members. Collective agents are social entities that are also rational agents. But the rational guidance they display is provided by the rational apparatus that governs the actions of the human beings who are their members.[16]

It should be emphasized that this conclusion is compatible with the assumption that human beings have moral reasons to create and maintain various social states of affairs, which will often be states of the social entities of which they are members. In this sense, there can be moral reasons for social entities to take a particular form. But the agents who act on these reasons will be human beings, in most cases the members of the social entity in question. The morally important social values mentioned earlier provide examples of moral reasons for a social entity to be a certain way. The social entity in that case is a state or polity. Thus there is a moral reason for the rule of law to obtain within a state or polity, but the agents who must act on this reason are the human beings who constitute the members of the state or polity. Similar points can be made about the legal reasons for corporations to be a certain way, for example, to possess a certain organizational structure. These are, ultimately, reasons for human beings who respect the law to perform certain actions.

The moral dimension of corporate management is not, then, determined by what social entities of a particular kind have sufficient reason to do. It is determined by what the associated human beings have sufficient reason to do. When we speak of the moral reasons for action possessed by a corporation, we must be understood as speaking of the moral reasons possessed by a collective agent, a set of human beings cooperating to achieve various results.

2

LEGITIMACY: THE PRIVATE MODEL

I HAVE SPOKEN of the exercise of subordinating authority by people acting on behalf of a collective agent. But authority relations can take another form, one unconnected to collective agency. Individuals functioning in a private capacity can enter into relations in which one party undertakes to comply with the directives of another. Certain kinds of employment usually involve such private authority relations—for example, the employment by a homeowner of a housekeeper, gardener, or handyman. The exercise of authority in such contexts, the deference by the employee to the directives of the employer, is a private matter located within the space that morality creates for individuals to live distinctive lives of which they are the authors.

It may also be possible to understand in this way the authority exercised by the owner of a small business. The ownership and management of a small business—a store, for example—can be as private, morally, as any other aspect of an individual's life. Many more laws govern the operation of a small business than govern most aspects of an individual's life, but this does not affect the possibility of placing the authority relations associated with a small business on a foundation provided by private morality. Conceivably a whole economy could be made up of such small, morally private enterprises.

The mechanism of private morality that seems most suitable for establishing an authority relation is consent. In general, consent is a normative mechanism by which one agent gives another a right to interact with him or her in a certain way. The most familiar examples are medical: the patient gives the doctor the right to perform certain procedures. When consent creates an authority relation, the right conferred is a right to issue directives.

It might be thought that managerial authority in a large corporation can similarly be understood as grounded in consent. The employees consent to direction by men and women acting on behalf of the corporation. Talk of direction in corporate contexts does not presuppose a sharply hierarchical organizational structure. The issuing of directives can take the form of the establishment of goals that teams of employees are responsible for meeting on their own.[1]

Consent to direction can be understood more specifically as involving a promise to comply with the directives emanating from some source. In the case of employment, the promise is made in return for a reciprocal promise by the employer to compensate compliance. If the authority of the executives of a large corporation can be provided with a foundation of this sort, there will be a basis for understanding it as a morally private matter.

I am going to reject this suggestion. To be more precise, I am going to argue that a promissory obligation to comply with managerial directives in return for pay cannot place the subordinating authority exercised by the senior executives of a large corporation on a secure foundation. Because of the effect that the actions of large a corporation can have on the public good, a promissory obligation to comply with managerial directives in return for pay can come into conflict with other important

33

moral considerations, and these may be capable of outweighing the obligation. If managerial authority is to be provided with a secure foundation, it must rather be understood as a lower-level form of political authority like that exercised by the heads of governmental departments or agencies, or by state governments in a federal system.

In arguing that a promissory obligation is not capable of supplying an adequate foundation for the authority exercised by corporate executives, this book assumes that a foundation of some sort is required. The book assumes that authority must be legitimate. It is a feature of our modern Western understanding of social relations that people receiving directives in institutional contexts must have sufficient reason, beyond that provided by the threat of penalties, for complying with the directives.

It might be replied that the need for legitimacy arises only in connection with government. The issuing of directives, in the sense relevant to authority relations, plays no role in the economic life of a capitalist society. All we have is market exchanges, some of which involve the trading of actions for money. It is possible to construct a picture of a capitalist economy that takes this form.[2] But regardless of the merits of such a view as an exercise in economic theorizing, accepting it involves assuming that the only important consideration in assessing the economic activity is economic efficiency. As I indicated in the Introduction, the argument that follows rejects this assumption. It takes other morally relevant effects of economic activity into account as well.

When employees are sensitive to these other effects, they may find participation in corporate cooperation problematic because it involves contributing to outcomes they judge to be morally objectionable. Similarly, citizens may find participation in political cooperation problematic because it involves contributing to outcomes, those associated with the government's policies,

that they judge to be morally objectionable. Under such circumstances, the achievement of cooperation normally requires
a willingness on the part of the members of the relevant group
to comply, within limits, with directives that seem ill-advised
or positively mistaken. Deference of this kind is the essence of
subordinating authority.[3] The fact that, intuitively, employment
involves such deference lends support to the idea that corporate
activity has moral consequences that are not captured by the
notion of economic efficiency.

My goal in this chapter is to explain more fully why a promise to comply with managerial directives in return for pay is not
capable of providing the authority exercised by corporate executives with a secure foundation.

Employees as Agents

If we take the legitimacy of managerial authority to be
grounded in a promise, to whom is the promise made? In simple
cases of domestic employment like those described earlier, the
promise is made to a human being who is engaged in a pursuit
that morality protects because it forms part of a distinctive life
of which he or she is the author. In corporate contexts, by contrast, the employer is the corporation itself. How should a promise to comply with managerial directives be understood in this
case?

In the law, employees are typically viewed as agents of their
employers. According to the *Restatement (Third) of Agency*, "[A]n
employee is an agent whose principal controls or has the right
to control the manner and means of the agent's performance of
work."[4] The contrast is with an independent contractor, whose
manner and means of performance are not, in theory anyway,
controlled by the person retaining his services. The *Restatement*
characterizes agency more particularly as "the fiduciary rela-

tionship that arises when one person (a 'principal') manifests assent to another person (an 'agent') that the agent shall act on the principal's behalf and subject to the principal's control, and the agent manifests assent or otherwise consents so to act."[5] "A person is (a) an individual; (b) an organization or association that has the legal capacity to possess rights and incur obligations; (c) a government, political subdivision, or instrumentality or entity created by government; or (d) any other entity that has legal capacity to possess rights and incur obligations."[6] Further, "[a]n agent has a duty to comply with all lawful instructions received from the principal and persons designated by the principal concerning the agent's actions on behalf of the principal."[7] From the standpoint of the law, then, the employees of a corporation have consented to a kind of authority relation. The executives of the corporation will be among those designated by the corporate principal to issue directives to its employees.

We are concerned, however, with the conditions under which corporate executives can claim to be exercising legitimate subordinating authority, and legitimate subordinating authority is not simply a matter of legal relations. As mentioned earlier, it presupposes a normative framework that is independent of the law. Considerations of legitimacy, understood as grounded in such a framework, guide the thinking of the members of a polity about how to structure their legal system. The use of the agency model in a political theory of the corporation thus requires that we find some normative basis independent of the law for regarding employees as agents of the corporate principal. The possibility we are now considering is that the moral mechanism of promising can provide this.

It will be useful to expand briefly on these points. If employees have a legal obligation to comply with lawful instructions from their employers, it might seem possible to give a simple and direct argument that corporate executives exercise legitimate subordinating authority over employees. As explained more fully in Chapter 3, when a government possesses legitimate authority within a population, most members of the population will have sufficient nonlegal reason to obey the law. So where political authority is legitimate, most employees of a corporation will have sufficient nonlegal reason to discharge their legal obligations as agents, including their obligation to comply with lawful instructions. It follows that those issuing the instructions, ultimately the senior executives, will be exercising legitimate authority within the corporation.

But this top-down way of establishing the legitimacy of the subordinating authority exercised by the leaders of subgroups in a larger population gives us no insight into why these authority relations should obtain in the first place, and thus no insight into why the law should be structured so as to support them. To gain this insight, we have to identify a normative consideration that is operative in the contexts in question and capable of providing a justification that is independent of the law for complying with the relevant directives.

When the parties are moral persons, a promise, understood as giving rise to a moral obligation, suffices to underwrite an agency relation. But in Chapter 1, I argued that corporations cannot be regarded as moral persons, which means that moral obligations cannot be owed to them. It might appear to follow immediately that managerial authority in a large corporation cannot be understood as a private matter. A corporation, as such, cannot be the recipient of a promise that creates a genuine moral obligation. Still, the idea that employment in a corporation involves a promise to comply with managerial directives in return for pay has some intuitive plausibility. We can explain this, without viewing corporations as moral persons, if we understand the promise as being made not to the corporation itself but to the people comprising the corporation.

The suggestion becomes more plausible if we bear in mind that there is a close connection between making a promise to do something and inducing someone to rely on one's doing it.[8] Intentionally inducing reliance on one's performing a particular action is often thought to give rise to an obligation to perform it, and this obligation structures interaction in a way similar to the way it is structured by a promissory obligation. Thus if I intentionally induce the members of a group to rely on my taking them to a football game—by, for example, saying that I plan to do this—in important respects, the situation will have the same normative structure as one in which I explicitly promise to take them. I will be acting wrongly if I fail to do what I have led these people to expect that I will do. It seems clear that in accepting employment in a corporation, an individual induces the other members of the corporation to rely on his doing his job, where this includes doing what he is told to do by superiors, as long as he is paid. Further, this situation is general within the corporation. All the members of a corporation will have induced one another to rely on their doing their jobs as long as they are paid.

A corporation cannot be the holder of any moral rights. But all its members, the senior executives as well as ordinary employees, will rely on one another to do their jobs, as specified by the organizational structure of the corporation, and this mutual reliance will give rise to an interlocking set of obligations not to disappoint reliance. This set of obligations can be regarded as functionally equivalent to a set of promissory obligations, owed to the corporation, to act as its agent in return for pay, and instructions received from designated superiors can be seen as having been issued by the corporation itself. The provision of pay by the corporation can be given a similar interpretation. It will involve the dispensing of corporate property by employees who are performing their assigned tasks.[9]

Two points of clarification are necessary before we proceed. First, in the law, employees are distinguished from independent contractors, and temporary employees are often understood as independent contractors. But the argument that follows applies to temporary employees as well as to employees of the standard sort. Both are recipients of directives, which may be merely goal setting, from senior executives and other managers. And the moral considerations that challenge, and that support, complying with these directives are the same for both.

Second, understood in the way I have proposed, the moral obligations associated with employment are not in fact promissory. They derive rather from the induction of reliance. But for simplicity, in what follows I will continue to speak of the obligation of private morality that employees have to comply with managerial directives as a promissory obligation incurred upon accepting employment. The question we now face is whether this obligation can justify compliance by employees with managerial directives.

The Normative Duality of Management

In Chapter 1, I mentioned de facto authority, the ability to get the members of a collective agent to do certain things simply by directing them to do these things. But I also said that in the normal case, the threat of a penalty of some sort for noncompliance will play a role in the exercise of subordinating authority. The general ability to get the members of a collective agent to do certain things by directing them to do these things, with or without the threat of a penalty for noncompliance, can be termed *directive power*. Directive power contrasts with legitimate authority. Directive power is a social fact, but legitimate subordinating authority has a normative dimension. Where legitimate authority exists, the recipients of directives have a reason to comply that transcends the de facto configuration of social power and, in particular, that transcends the ability of the source of directives to punish noncompliance.

De facto authority can be grounded in the possession of charisma or the existence in the recipients of a habit of obedience so that they are disposed to "respect authority." The most important source of de facto authority, however, is a belief on the part of the people receiving direction that the person or entity issuing the directives possesses legitimate authority—that he, she, or it has a right, or license of some other kind, to issue them. Of course, this belief may be false, but if it exists, it can prompt compliance with the directives.

This last point applies to my project here. As I have said, I am going to argue that the legitimacy of managerial authority cannot be grounded in a promissory, or quasi-promissory, obligation to comply with managerial directives in return for pay. But many employees may believe that they have an obligation of this kind to do what their bosses tell them to do, and this may give the bosses de facto authority. It is compatible with the legitimacy of a particular authority relation that the subordinates have an erroneous understanding of what establishes its legitimacy. All that is necessary is that the conditions of legitimacy actually obtain. But a correct understanding of these conditions is desirable. There are limits on what legitimate authorities can require the people over whom they exercise authority to do, and an awareness of these limits on the part of the subordinates can help ensure that they are respected.

Corporate executives, then, may possess de facto authority within the groups they manage. But they also possess directive power of the other sort, the sort grounded in the ability to penalize noncompliance. Executives are legally authorized to exercise corporate property rights, and this gives them the ability to threaten a penalty, the termination of employment, for noncompliance. The termination of employment has the consequence that the employee will no longer be receiving pay, and the threat of this may induce compliance. It also involves the exclusion of the employee from the premises of the employer, which constitutes an additional exercise of property rights.

The fact that executives are authorized to exercise corporate property rights might seem to offer us a different way of grounding managerial authority in private right. In accepting the existence of nongovernmental corporations that engage in productive activities, a society is accepting private ownership of productive resources. This is legal ownership, but in general people have a moral reason to respect legal property rights. It might thus be claimed that the moral reason employees have to respect corporate property rights justifies their compliance with managerial directives.

We can speak here of the thesis of the normative unity of management. If managerial authority is to be legitimately exercised, the people running the corporation must have a license to issue directives to the employees. There must be some normative consideration, independent of a penalty for noncompliance, that establishes that there is sufficient reason for the employees to comply with managerial directives. Executives and other managers also need a license to manipulate the productive property associated with the corporation. They have this license because they are authorized, by virtue of the organizational roles they occupy, to exercise corporate property rights. But it might be thought that because employees have a moral reason to respect legal property rights, this second license is at the same time a license to issue directives to employees. This would establish that management possesses a normative unity. A single normative consideration would ground both of the licenses required to operate a business.

In fact, however, we must accept the normative duality of

41

management.[10] Property rights cannot ground a license on the part of managers to tell employees what to do. To be more precise, they cannot ground a license that is sufficient for the purposes of management. Property rights bring with them what might be called a negative right to direct the actions of others. An owner can require other people to *refrain* from interacting in specific ways with his property, but ownership does not give an owner a right to direct other people to interact in specific ways with his property. My ownership of my car gives me the right to tell someone who is driving it to refrain from certain courses of action, but it does not give me the right to direct her to drive it someplace. If she refuses to drive it where I want, I can order her out of the car. So if she wants to stay in the car, she will have a nonmoral reason, a reason of self-interest, to comply with my directives. But my property rights do not give her a further, moral, reason to comply, any more than they would give a passerby a reason to comply with a directive to get into the car and drive it someplace. Property rights can create *directive power* when their exercise meshes in a certain way with the desires or needs of other people, but they do not give an owner a moral license to order another person actively to manipulate his property.[11]

It may be helpful to look at another example. My ownership of my house and its contents gives visitors a moral reason to refrain from interacting with them in ways that I specify. If I tell a visitor not to sit in a certain antique chair, she will have a moral reason not to sit in it. But my property rights do not give a visitor a moral reason to comply with a directive to change a light bulb. If I direct a visitor to do this and she refuses, I can order her out of the house. So if she does not want to be ordered out—perhaps it's cold outside—she will have a self-interested reason to change the light bulb. But my property rights will not give her a moral reason to change it.

These points are straightforwardly applicable to corporate management. The fact that senior executives and other managers are authorized to exercise corporate property rights gives them directive power over their subordinates. Employees typically do not want to lose their jobs. But property rights cannot provide a moral basis for managerial authority, a license to tell the employees what to do. Because managers are authorized to exercise corporate property rights, employees have a moral reason to refrain from interacting with corporate property in ways that management forbids. But something other than a property right is needed to establish that employees have a moral reason, or justification of some other kind that transcends the threat of penalties, for performing the positive actions that their bosses direct them to perform.[12]

43

The management of a corporation thus requires two licenses, a license to manipulate the productive property associated with the corporation and a separate license to direct the actions of the employees. We can now turn to the question of whether this second license can be provided by a promissory, or quasi-promissory, obligation to comply with managerial directives in return for pay.

Promising and Legitimacy

The main problem with the idea that the legitimacy of subordinating authority can be grounded in a promissory obligation, or indeed in any substantive moral reason for action, is that substantive moral reasons for action can be outweighed by other moral considerations. The possibility that promissory obligations, in particular, can be outweighed is familiar in moral philosophy. The hackneyed example concerns someone who has promised to attend a party but encounters a serious automobile accident on the way and is uniquely able to render assistance to the victims.

A promissory obligation to comply with directives can usually justify compliance when the recipient has self-interested reasons for doing something else. It is central to the distinctive role played by morality in human life that moral reasons for action ordinarily take precedence over reasons of self-interest. But when someone who has promised to comply with directives has a *moral* reason for doing something else, he may be able to conclude that this reason outweighs his promissory obligation. Suppose that Smith has promised to comply with somebody's directives, and that person directs him to drive to a warehouse at a particular time. If Smith encounters a serious automobile accident on the way and is uniquely able to render assistance to the victims, it may be permissible for him to break the promise. In such a case, the right to compliance created by the promise will be suspended.

The possibility of conflict between a promissory obligation and a moral reason to do something else can also arise for the employees of a corporation. An employee who has a promissory, or quasi-promissory, obligation to comply with managerial directives may be directed to act in a way that he regards as morally objectionable. If so, he will have to decide which of the conflicting moral considerations has greater weight in the circumstances. We must be clear about the nature of this decision, however.

If bosses are able to punish employees for noncompliance, with the termination of employment or in other ways, employees will have a self-interested reason to comply with the directives they receive, a reason that, it might seem, can be added to the moral reason provided by the promissory obligation. But the existence of such self-interested reasons has no bearing on what morality requires, and it is what morality requires that counts when the license to issue directives is understood as a moral license. A self-interested reason may succeed in producing compliance in a situation where the moral reason for compliance is judged to be outweighed. But when that is the case, the employee, if conscientious, will have the uneasy feeling that he is doing, or going along with, something morally wrong because the personal sacrifice involved in acting on his moral convictions would be too great. We can imagine Smith having such feelings if he leaves the scene of the accident, despite being uniquely able to render assistance, because he is afraid of losing his job. Effective control established in this way is not the same thing as legitimate authority.

These observations play an important role in the argument that follows. The next two sections are concerned with whether the promissory obligation that we are assuming employees to incur in accepting employment—an obligation to comply with managerial directives in return for pay—is sufficient to establish the legitimacy of the authority exercised by corporate executives and other managers. In investigating this question, we must be careful to distinguish the moral reason provided by this obligation from reasons of other kinds that employees may have for complying with the directives they receive. The discussion in this section focuses on what can be accomplished with a promissory obligation to comply with managerial directives. The discussion in the next section brings back into the picture the fact that the employee is being paid for complying.

We are exploring the possibility that a promissory obligation to comply with managerial directives can be outweighed by moral objections to what an employee is directed to do. A natural response is that although this may be true in the abstract, it is irrelevant in practice because employees are rarely directed to do anything morally objectionable. Skeptics about the moral character of profit-seeking corporations may disagree. But if we are talking about directives to violate requirements of private morality, the reply has some plausibility, at least in reputable corporations. At any rate, I am going to assume that employees are not directed by their bosses to perform actions like cheating people. Moreover, it will, I think, be conceded that a promissory obligation to comply with managerial directives would not be able to justify the performance of such actions.

There are other ways a directed action can seem morally questionable, however, and these require more careful examination. To see this, we must broaden our understanding of what constitutes a moral consideration. In modern societies, many people regard the maintenance of certain social states of affairs or the securing of certain social outcomes as possessing moral importance independently of whether maintaining or securing them is supported by the requirements governing interaction among individuals. These morally important social values were described in Chapter 1. Examples include distributive justice, the rule of law, social prosperity, the preservation of the environment, the fostering of community, the maintenance of the health of the population, the advancement of knowledge, the development of culture, and the defense of the country.

As described at greater length in the following chapters, profit-seeking corporations can make an important contribution to a polity's overall effort to promote the morally important social values. But corporate actions can also negatively affect this effort. Profit-seeking corporations have strong incentives to take steps that reduce costs or increase revenue, and taking these steps can sometimes be judged to have negative consequences for various morally important social values. One important example in the United States concerns managerial resistance to the unionization of the workforce, which could be perceived as subverting the value of distributive justice.[13] Other examples include a policy in a medical insurance company of denying a fixed percentage of claims, efforts by pharmaceutical companies to encourage the use of expensive drugs when equally effective generic alternatives are available, the aggressive marketing by food companies of tasty but unhealthy snacks, and efforts by energy companies to maintain or expand environmentally irresponsible practices. Corporate actions of these kinds could be judged to have negative effects on the health of the population or on the environment.

A somewhat different example is provided by the efforts of a **47** defense contractor to expand or preserve the production of a weapons system designed for military conditions that no longer obtain. This could be judged to have a negative effect on the value of national defense. Also noteworthy are industry-wide practices that may be followed by relatively small companies, such as the extensive use of antibiotics in animals intended for food. This could be perceived as having a negative impact on the health of the human population that consumes the food. [14]

The recent financial crisis has made us familiar with another important example, the marketing of financial products of various kinds to people whose acceptance of them will leave them with too much debt. As has now become clear, this can have disastrous consequences for the prosperity of the society as a whole. This example shows that the pursuit of profit in a market context does not automatically promote even the value of social prosperity, much less the public good generally. The relation between the pursuit of profit and the promotion of social prosperity is explored at greater length in Chapters 4 and 5.

In the examples just described, the detrimental consequences for the morally important social values stem from what might be called direct efforts to increase revenue or reduce costs. But indirect efforts to achieve these goals—for example, by lobbying for legislation or regulation that is more accommodating of direct efforts—can also be seen as compromising the promotion of morally important social values. Thus lobbying by banks for lower capital requirements, which would enable individual banks to make more money, could be perceived as morally problematic if the lowering itself would threaten social prosperity. Similar points can be made about public relations campaigns designed to create support for direct efforts to increase revenue or reduce costs.

In a variety of ways, then, the steps that corporations take to increase profits or reduce costs might be judged morally objectionable because of their effects on morally important social values. But is this fact sufficient to call into question the possibility of grounding managerial authority in a promissory obligation? The argument that follows does not attempt to show that a promissory obligation is never able to justify compliance with managerial directives. The aim is rather to raise doubts about whether a promissory obligation can justify compliance effectively enough to place the legitimacy of managerial authority on a secure normative foundation. This will set the stage for the next chapter, in which I argue that we can provide a more secure foundation for the legitimacy of managerial authority by viewing it as a species of political authority.

We begin with two preliminary points. First, managerial directives sustain the corporation as a collective agent. By complying with the directives they receive from their bosses, employees at all levels play a role in producing any negative consequences attributable to the actions or policies of their corporation. This means that the question we are considering arises for all corporate employees. They all must decide whether their promissory obligation to comply with managerial directives is outweighed by the fact that the actions or policies of their corporation have morally objectionable features. Second, the argument assumes that the corporate actions or policies in question are legal. However, actions that are legal can still be judged morally impermissible. The fact that questions of political morality admit of reasonable disagreement makes it especially likely that there will be perceived disparities between law and morality.

The argument that raises doubts about whether a promissory obligation can place managerial authority on a secure foundation has three steps. The first step involves identifying a general way an individual could have a moral reason to decline to participate in a collective endeavor that she regards as possessing morally objectionable features. She could see such participation as compromising her moral integrity. The significance, for our purposes, of the concept of moral integrity is that the preservation of integrity can give an individual a strong reason for action even where the degree of causal responsibility for a morally objectionable outcome is relatively minor. The basic idea is that one may judge oneself to be, so to speak, soiled morally by involvement with certain activities, and this can provide a strong moral reason for disengagement regardless of one's degree of causal responsibility. Thus the preservation of moral integrity can provide a strong reason for declining to purchase clothing made in a sweatshop even though that particular act will have no discernable impact on what happens there.[15]

Similarly, the preservation of moral integrity can give an employee who judges morally objectionable certain actions or policies of her corporation a strong reason to decline to contribute to those actions by complying with managerial directives. This will be true regardless of whether she is directly involved in the specific parts of the corporate effort that she finds problematic. Further, such reasons for disengagement need not be grounded in a judgment that the corporation's activities, taken as a whole, are having a negative impact on the public good. The perception that particular corporate actions or policies are morally objectionable can be enough to justify a given employee in concluding that she is soiled morally by continuing to work for the corporation.

It might seem that, in such a case, the employee should quit. The promise to comply with managerial directives is a promise to comply in return for pay, so an employee who has made such a promise will not be doing anything morally wrong by quitting, thereby foregoing pay. But many employees in the situation we are considering will not have this option. They will need to keep their jobs to support themselves or their families. This means that they will be forced by circumstances to compromise their integrity. A case of this sort must be distinguished from one in which an agent simply surrenders her integrity by succumbing to a temptation. As mentioned in Chapter 1, a morally responsible agent may decline to make the sacrifices required by morally important social values when making them would mean abandoning commitments and pursuits that contribute to the meaningfulness of her life. And keeping one's job can be necessary for the maintenance of such commitments and pursuits. So an employee in a situation of the kind we are envisaging could be permitted, morally, to keep her job.

However, it does not follow from the fact that the employee is permitted to keep her job that the reason of integrity she has for disengagement is nullified. It is bypassed by her need to make a living, but it remains capable of exerting its force in other ways. This has implications for the possibility of grounding the legitimacy of the authority exercised over an employee in a promissory obligation to comply with managerial directives. If the authority is to be legitimately exercised, the promissory obligation must be capable of outweighing any reasons of integrity for not complying.[16]

We should be clear about how the argument works here. We are assuming that in accepting employment, an employee incurs a promissory, or quasi-promissory, obligation to comply with managerial directives in return for pay. This obligation will remain in force as long as she remains in her job. Further, as we have seen, an employee for whom quitting on moral grounds would mean a serious loss may be permitted, morally, to remain in her job. But the permission does not strengthen the obligation.

The two considerations point in the same direction, but they operate independently of each other, at different moral levels.

In the same way, the permission the employee has to remain in her job does not nullify her reason of integrity for quitting. The two considerations operate independently of each other at different moral levels but this time to opposite effect. The employee acts on the permission and continues to comply with managerial directives. But the reason of integrity retains its force, waiting for an opportunity to assert itself. And it gets such an opportunity because it conflicts with the promissory obligation to comply with managerial directives, potentially defeating the obligation. If reasons of integrity did not work this way, employers could nullify the threat such reasons can pose to the legitimacy of their authority simply by restricting their hiring to people for whom quitting would be too costly.

An example of a situation of the sort we have been considering is the case of a chemical company that fights regulation designed to reduce the risk of an accidental discharge of dangerous chemicals, or a discharge produced by a terrorist attack, that would threaten the health of neighboring populations. Some competently reasoning employees of the company may judge that they are soiled morally by working for a company that acts in this way and, as a result, conclude that they have a reason of integrity for quitting. But they may also find it necessary to keep their jobs, and thus to comply with managerial directives, in order to support their families. The permission, or prerogative, to decline to take actions justified by morally important social values, when this would mean sacrificing central commitments or pursuits, will justify such employees in keeping their jobs. But this does not alter the fact that in doing so they will be compromising their integrity. The moral obstacle that reasons of integrity can place in the way of discharging a promissory obligation will thus remain, potentially defeating the obligation to comply with managerial directives. When this happens—when the obligation is defeated—the employees will still comply with the directives they receive, but their doing so will not be justified by the promissory obligation. The obligation will not give those issuing the directives the requisite license. These people will simply be exercising directive power.

As explained in Chapter 1, the permission, or prerogative, we are discussing is a permission to resist the demands of consequentialist considerations like the morally important social values. Moral agents have no prerogative to decline to make sacrifices arising from the requirements of private morality. So if an employee is directed to violate a requirement of private morality—to cheat someone, for example—she morally must refuse, challenging her employer to fire her. Similar points apply to directives to break the law.

It is, then, only with respect to corporate activities that are legal and are perceived to have negative consequences for morally important social values that we find a situation of the kind we are now exploring. It is only in such cases that an employee can (1) be justified by exigent needs in complying with managerial directives despite the fact that she takes herself, in doing so, to be compromising her moral integrity, and yet (2) precisely because she takes her integrity to be compromised, judge her promissory obligation to comply with the directives to be outweighed.

The second step of the argument involves the phenomenon of reasonable moral disagreement. The members of a corporation can be expected to disagree about whether contributing to corporate cooperation presents issues of integrity. Some may not see the problems others do. And those who think that corporate cooperation does present issues of integrity can be expected to disagree about whether the resulting reason for action is strong enough to defeat a promissory obligation on the other side.

Moreover, these disagreements could be reasonable in the sense that the conclusions reached could all be competently reasoned. To establish the ultimate significance of considerations of integrity for the legitimacy of managerial authority, then, we need to delve more deeply into the way that reasonable moral disagreement bears on legitimacy.

Reasonable disagreement about issues of political morality is possible because the different life experiences of the members of a polity can give them different perspectives on the moral reasons that are relevant to the organization of political cooperation. As a result, when they reason competently about how cooperation morally ought to be organized, they reach different conclusions. The conclusions that the competently reasoning members of a polity could reach on a particular issue of political morality constitute what I call the *zone of reasonable disagreement* surrounding that issue.

The zone of reasonable disagreement has a counterfactual aspect. It does not consist of the set of positions on a given issue that we find the members of a polity actually taking. It consists of the set of positions they would take if they reasoned competently, within their different perspectives on the relevant reasons. Competent reasoning is facilitated by shared deliberation with those who hold opposing views. So the zone of reasonable disagreement surrounding a particular issue of political morality can also be understood as the set of positions that would survive shared deliberation conducted in good faith over an extended period of time. One can reason competently on the basis of incomplete information. But for the characterization of the zone of reasonable disagreement, we should understand the parties to the disagreement to possess all relevant information. Shared deliberation can help to ensure that this condition is satisfied.

It is important to note that reasonable disagreement is a form of disagreement. All the contending positions are reasonable in the sense that they can be supported by competent reasoning. But they will usually not be seen as reasonable by those holding opposing positions.[17] A party to a reasonable disagreement will normally see the reasoning supporting positions other than her own as in some way flawed.

In modern societies, much controversy exists about whether the actions and policies of profit-seeking corporations are having a detrimental effect on the public good, and it is plausible that these controversies contain a core of reasonable disagreement. In general, the members of a modern society will have different perspectives, shaped by their different life experiences, on the reasons relevant to questions concerning the public good. They will thus, even when reasoning competently, generate different answers to these questions. Further, it can be expected that this disagreement will be replicated to a certain extent within any corporation whose actions and policies are controversial in the larger society. The employees of a large corporation will be drawn from many different segments of society and will carry the perspectives on the relevant reasons associated with those segments into the corporation. So when the question whether a corporation's actions and policies are compatible with the public good admits of reasonable disagreement within the society as a whole, it is likely that it will also admit of reasonable disagreement, to some extent, among the corporation's employees.

It requires emphasis that we are envisaging competent moral reasoning carried out within the perspectives on the relevant reasons provided by the life experiences of a corporation's employees. Competent moral reasoning must be distinguished from the rationalization of a course of action that is in one's interest. This is discussed in more detail later in this chapter, in the section "Self-Interest and Corporate Policy."

Controversies of the kind we are now considering are not restricted to a few high-profile industries. The news often contains stories reporting a problem of public significance apparently caused by the activities of some corporation or the practices of some industry, together with proposed remedies. Just as often, the stories go on to describe resistance to the proposed remedies by corporate executives or industry spokespersons, who deny that the problem is as serious as reported or who argue that the proposed remedies would be too costly for them, for consumers, or for the public generally. The point here is not that corporate executives or industry spokespersons always put profit ahead of the public good. Rather, it is that such controversies often contain a core of reasonable disagreement, which we can expect would be replicated to some extent within the corporations in question if the employees were reasoning competently.

In summary, many of the moral issues concerning corporate policy in a modern capitalist society admit of reasonable disagreement. Competent moral reasoning will yield different, incompatible conclusions. This makes it likely that some employees of a corporation whose policies are controversial in the larger society would, if reasoning competently within the framework of their life experiences, judge the policies morally unacceptable. But then our earlier argument comes into play. Some employees in this group may conclude that they nevertheless have sufficient reason to comply with managerial directives because their promissory obligation to comply is weightier than the opposing considerations, but others may come to the opposite conclusion. They may conclude, possibly on grounds of integrity, as explained earlier, that the opposing considerations are weightier than the obligation. For these employees, corporate executives and other managers will possess only directive power.

The third, and final, step of the argument concerns the significance of the disagreement we have been envisaging for managerial legitimacy. It is not realistic to require, as a condition of the legitimate exercise of subordinating authority over the members of a collective agent, that every member be able to judge, when reasoning competently, that something beyond the threat of penalties justifies compliance with the associated directives. Eccentric reasoning—for example, the reasoning of philosophically sophisticated anarchists—can be competent. But the number of members in this situation must be a very small percentage of the total. When the number is relatively large, the source of the directives will not be able to claim legitimate authority within the group as a whole. Thus in the political case, when a substantial number of the residents of a state (a country) find themselves unable to judge, as competent reasoners, that they have sufficient reason, independent of coercive sanctions, to comply with the directives they are receiving from the government, the legitimacy of the government is called into question.[18] A police state, where order is maintained only by coercion, would be an extreme example.

It is doubtful that a precise threshold can be established here—for instance, a requirement that at least 99 percent of the citizens of a state be able, as competent reasoners, to judge that they have sufficient, coercion-independent reason, to comply with the official directives of the state. Rather there is a sliding scale of legitimacy. As the number of competently reasoning citizens for whom only the threat of punishment justifies complying with the official directives of the state grows larger, it becomes increasingly doubtful that the government can claim to be exercising legitimate authority. And when a substantial number of citizens are in this situation, legitimacy is lost.

Legitimacy becomes increasingly doubtful under these circumstances because the function of subordinating authority, exercised over the members of a collective agent, is to secure coordinated action by the members. A little bit of slippage at the edges can be tolerated. But if there are substantial gaps in the cooperative effort that would be produced by justified compliance with the directives issued by a putative authority, the ability of justified compliance to perform this coordinating function will be compromised. Legitimacy will thus be called into question.

The distinction between legitimate authority and directive power must be borne in mind here. By the application of directive power—for example, threats of punishment for noncompliance—a putative authority may be able to close the gaps that would otherwise be present. But a source of directives will have a clear claim to legitimate authority over the members of a collective agent only if almost all have sufficient reason, independent of the application of directive power to them personally, to comply with the directives they are receiving.[19]

Applied to the corporate case, these observations give us the following result. When the employees of a corporation have only self-interested reasons for declining to comply with managerial directives, a promissory obligation to comply is usually enough to ensure that the directives will be able to perform their coordinating function. But when the employees have moral reasons, including reasons of integrity, for declining to comply, the situation is more problematic. The reasons for declining to comply may defeat the promissory obligation. The earlier argument makes it plausible that some employees of a large corporation, if reasoning competently about the relevant moral requirements, would find themselves in this situation. They would judge a promissory obligation to comply with managerial directives to be defeated by opposing moral considerations. And this raises the question whether the executives of a large corporation can be understood as exercising legitimate authority within the corporation as a whole.[20]

The answer need not always be negative. In a particular corporation, the number of employees who would judge the obligation to be defeated, were they reasoning competently, might be small enough that there would be no significant gaps in the cooperative effort produced by justified compliance with managerial directives. But equally, the gaps could be so large that corporate executives cannot be understood as exercising legitimate authority. So when the authority that executives exercise over employees is grounded in a promissory obligation, we are left with *uncertainty* about the legitimacy of this authority. In any given corporation, legitimacy may be lacking.

What we need, then, is a way of establishing the legitimacy of the subordinating authority exercised by corporate executives that is less susceptible to the idiosyncrasies of the experience of particular employees, and to the idiosyncrasies of policy of particular corporations, than the one we have been exploring. If such a way of establishing legitimacy can be found, we should make any changes in our understanding of the nature of managerial authority that it may require.

The role of reasonable moral disagreement in this argument deserves emphasis. We can expect reasonable disagreement among the employees of a large corporation about whether the corporation's actions and policies are having a detrimental effect on particular morally important social values. We can also expect reasonable disagreement about whether a promissory obligation to comply with managerial directives is capable of defeating any moral considerations that may point in the other direction. This means that *there is no single correct answer to these questions*, no single answer that competent moral reasoning would inevitably produce. But precisely because there is no single correct answer, it is plausible that some employees of a large corporation, if reasoning competently, would judge the promissory obligation to be defeated. And this introduces the doubt whose implications we have been exploring.

It bears repeating that there may be corporations where a promissory obligation is capable of grounding the legitimacy of managerial authority. In fact, there may be corporations where none of the employees, proceeding competently within their distinctive perspectives on the relevant reasons, would find anything morally objectionable about corporate policy. But it would be difficult to identify these corporations. And we would still need a solution for the remaining corporations. In Chapter 3, I propose a way of establishing the legitimacy of managerial authority that is capable, in principle, of encompassing all the corporations in a capitalist society at once.[21]

The Receipt of Pay

It might seem that the argument so far has overlooked a decisive consideration, the fact that the employee is being paid for complying with managerial directives. Someone who has simply made a promise to comply with certain directives issued by another person—to do what a personal trainer tells him to do, for example—may be able to conclude that there are good moral reasons for breaking the promise. Perhaps merely pecking at the huge meal served by a well-meaning relative would be deeply insulting to her. But surely, it will be said, an employee cannot justifiably accept pay if he has not complied with managerial directives. Conversely, if he is going to accept pay, he has sufficient moral reason to comply.

It is true that under all but the most extraordinary circumstances, an employee cannot justifiably accept pay if he has failed to comply with managerial directives. But this does not alter the results we have obtained. An obligation to comply with directives in return for pay is a conditional obligation. If, at time $t1$, the employee expects the condition to be satisfied—if he believes that the employer will at a future time $t2$ provide the pay—he will at $t1$ have a moral reason of some particular strength to comply with the directives he receives. But he may still be able to judge that other moral reasons he has at $t1$ outweigh that moral reason.

The interesting question concerns what happens next. An employee who regards himself as morally justified, all things considered, in declining to comply with managerial directives and who, as a result, does not comply will have a moral reason to refuse any pay that might be offered in the future. To accept pay would be to defraud the employer. The employee has promised to comply with managerial directives in return for a reciprocal promise on the part of the employer to pay him if he complies.[22] If he accepts pay even though he has not complied, he will be exploiting the employer's ignorance of the fact that the condition specified for payment has not been satisfied. Moreover, if the employee is going to refuse pay in the future, he will normally have sufficient self-interested reason to leave his job—to quit.

These facts might seem to render much of the previous argument pointless. If an employee has moral reservations about what his employer is doing serious enough to outweigh his promissory obligation to comply with managerial directives, he ought to quit. Remaining would mean either defrauding the employer (if he is going to accept pay) or wasting his time (if he is going to refuse pay). And if he does not have such reservations, his promissory obligation will place managerial authority on a secure foundation. So if employees behave responsibly, the problematic situation in which executives and other managers possess directive power but not legitimate authority will never arise.

But things are not so simple. For many employees, quitting would involve a great personal sacrifice. They need their jobs to support themselves or a family. We saw in the previous section that this fact can force employees who regard their corporations as pursuing morally objectionable policies or as engaging in morally objectionable practices to compromise their integrity. It can force them to keep their jobs even though they regard themselves as soiled morally by working for a corporation that pursues those policies or engages in those practices. When this happens, the reasons of integrity remain in force, capable in principle of defeating any promissory obligation to comply with managerial directives.

The fact that employees have an obligation to comply with managerial directives in return for pay does not alter these conclusions. The employee will be doing something wrong if, assuming the employer's ignorance permits this, he accepts pay after failing to comply. He will be defrauding the employer. But it does not follow that he has a reason for complying with managerial directives of the kind that is required to establish the legitimacy of managerial authority.

An employee who has not complied with managerial directives will have a moral reason to deny himself pay if it is later offered. That is, he will have a moral reason to make a certain sacrifice. Further, the fact that the employee will have this moral reason in the future gives him a *self-interested* reason in the present to comply with the directives he receives. That way, he will be sparing himself the future sacrifice. But the requirement to avoid fraud provides no *moral* reason in the present to comply with the directives.

In effect, an employee in the situation we are considering has a moral reason to exercise on his employer's behalf the employer's directive power. In the normal case, an employer will not offer pay if an employee's failure to comply with the directives he has received has been detected, and this is the principal source of the employer's directive power—the employer's de facto ability to secure compliance. The moral reason an employee has to deny himself pay if he fails to comply simply establishes him as an agent of the employer in this respect. The employer will punish noncompliance with the suspension of pay or with termination, and the employee has a moral reason to punish himself in these ways if he does not comply, a reason stemming from the requirement to avoid fraud. Directive power, however, is not legitimate authority. So the moral reason the employee has to deny himself pay in case of noncompliance does not establish the legitimacy of managerial authority.

The normal situation of an employee who has moral reservations about what his employer is doing is thus the one described earlier. The employee will have the uneasy feeling that he is doing, or going along with, something morally objectionable because acting on his moral convictions would be too costly. But this means he will be responding only to directive power. The doubts raised above about whether a promissory obligation to comply with managerial directives can establish the legitimacy of managerial authority remain, then, even after we take into account that an employee who declines to comply cannot permissibly accept pay.[23]

Self-Interest and Corporate Policy

The argument presented in the two preceding sections assumes competent moral reasoning on the part of employees. This is important for the conclusions that have been reached regarding legitimate authority. When we hear that a dictator in some country has been returned to office by an overwhelming majority in a vote, we do not take this as establishing the dictator's legitimacy. One reason might be that the citizens have been subjected to indoctrination that has warped their thinking. Only judgments that reflect competent operation with the relevant reasons have a bearing on the legitimacy of authority. Applied to the corporate case, this gives us the result that to establish whether the senior executives of a large corporation are exercising legitimate authority over the employees, we must focus on the moral judgments the employees would make in the absence of psychological pressures that can distort reasoning.

It is possible that the employees of a corporation could be subjected to indoctrination of the sort that would compromise legitimacy. But the most important pressure that can distort the moral reasoning of corporate employees is the pressure of interest. It is often difficult, as a matter of psychological fact, to see that something responsible for one's livelihood is morally problematic, or if one does see this, to act accordingly.[24] When the pressure of interest is operative, the thinking that employees do about whether complying with managerial directives is morally justified may simply rationalize what is in their interest.

These points warrant further discussion. The results produced by rationalization will vary depending on what is in the interest of the people doing the thinking. But this phenomenon must be distinguished from reasonable disagreement. Reasonable disagreement about a question of political morality, a question about the right way of organizing some aspect of political cooperation, arises from the fact that their different life experiences can give the members of a polity different perspectives on the relevant reasons. The relevant reasons are identified by moral and political concepts, such as those specifying the morally important social values or the requirements of private morality, which are available to everyone in the polity. But because the members will have different perspectives on these reasons, *competent* reasoning can yield different conclusions concerning what the reasons require.

The rationalizations that result when reasoning is distorted by interest also use socially available moral and political concepts in judgments concerning the appropriate way of organizing political cooperation. But the use of the concepts is guided, at bottom, by a perception of what would be in the interest of a particular individual or group. In a sense, the conclusion that is to be reached is established in advance by this perception, with the reasoning taking the form of an effort to manipulate the relevant concepts to create the impression that the conclusion has rational support. I do not mean to suggest that this procedure is always followed with full self-consciousness. To speak of the reasoning as distorted is to imply that the people producing it do not fully appreciate that it is merely a tissue of rationalization.

64   These observations have the consequence that even if we find that almost all the employees of a corporation endorse its policies, we cannot automatically conclude that the executives possess legitimate authority within the corporation. If authority is to be legitimately exercised, compliance with the relevant directives must be supportable by reasoning that is competent. As has been mentioned, this idea is familiar when the issue is the legitimacy of government. But the point is of general significance, applying to any case in which we find widespread support for institutional arrangements that involve the exercise of directive power. So in the corporate case, if the reason to comply with managerial directives is understood to be provided by a promise, a given employee's judgment that no competing moral reasons outweigh the promise must be free of distortion by self-interest.

It may be helpful to approach these ideas from a different angle. In their recent book, *Animal Spirits*, George Akerlof and Robert Shiller cite studies showing that as long as employees judge that they are being fairly compensated, they tend to be loyal to, and share the values of, their employers.[25] If the values in question are what might be called business values, such as making a profit or increasing market share, it is easy to understand how the perception that compensation is fair could lead to the sharing of these values. The money the employees are paid will have been generated by their collective pursuit of the values, and in judging themselves to be fairly compensated for their parts in that pursuit, they will be implicitly endorsing it.

But if the perception that they are being fairly compensated causes the employees of a large corporation to endorse the *moral* decisions that are made by corporate executives, if it causes them to share the values of their employers in that sense, they are allowing themselves to be bought off, as moral reasoners, by their employers. A fair distribution of the proceeds may be the only relevant moral consideration in a small business. But a large corporation is a center of activity that can have a pronounced effect on the public good, and the fact that compensation is fair—that it fairly rewards contribution to the corporation's revenue stream, for example—does not guarantee that this effect will be positive. So a competently reasoned endorsement of the moral decisions made by corporate executives cannot be based on this consideration alone.

We have been discussing the possibility that the moral judgment of employees can be distorted by the pressure of self-interest. It is important to note, however, that valid moral considerations can support the interests of employees. Consider, for example, an energy company some of whose projects are negatively impacting the environment. It may be that abandoning those projects would force the company to reduce the workforce. This would presumably be contrary to the interests of the employees who lost their jobs. But the termination of employment can also mean treating people in ways that violate certain requirements of private morality, such as the requirement of nonmaleficence or the requirement of mutual aid. When this is the case, the affected employees will have a moral claim that conflicts with the preservation of the environment.

Moral problems of this sort have the following basic form. The promotion of a morally important social value will involve hurting people, or failing to help them, in ways that are significant from the standpoint of private morality. Thus to determine what would serve the public good, we must make a judgment about the relative importance of moral considerations of two fundamentally different kinds. These issues are discussed in more detail in Chapter 4. But here it can be noted that cases in which acting to promote a morally important social value means overriding a claim grounded in a requirement of private morality are especially likely to give rise to reasonable disagreement. It is especially likely that competent reasoners, proceeding within their distinctive perspectives on the relevant reasons, will come to different conclusions.

To return to our example, some employees may be able to conclude, through competent reasoning, that the public good would be served by the continuation of the projects, despite the cost to the environment. Because the pressure of interest would point in the same direction, however, an employee who came to this conclusion could also simply be rationalizing what would be in his interest. Where interests protected by a requirement of private morality are involved, then, it may be especially difficult to determine whether a judgment about what would serve the public good is grounded in sound moral reasoning. This contributes to the general uncertainty we have been exploring about whether a promissory obligation is capable of establishing the legitimacy of managerial authority.

It should be noted that when the promotion of a morally important social value justifies the violation of a requirement of private morality, it is still incumbent on the larger society to consider how the loss to the individuals affected can be mitigated. The costs of promoting the public good must be fairly distributed. I say something more about this in Chapter 4, in connection with the case where the laying off of employees is claimed to be justified as promoting economic efficiency and thus the value of social prosperity.

In this section, we examined the distinction between competent moral reasoning in corporate contexts and rationalization. It needs to be emphasized that no assumption is being made that competently reasoning employees will be saintly. The point is simply that when people are reasoning competently about moral matters, their thinking is not distorted by self-interest.

Conclusion

Let's take stock. It appears that some competently reasoning employees of large corporations will be able to conclude that a promissory, or quasi-promissory, obligation to comply with managerial directives in return for pay is defeated by opposing moral considerations. Moreover, this group could be of significant size. But the larger the number of employees who can judge that they have no reason, independent of the threat of termination, to comply with the directives they are receiving, the more doubtful it will be that the executives and other managers issuing those directives can be understood as exercising legitimate authority within the corporation as a whole.

As a general proposition, then, it is uncertain whether the legitimacy of managerial authority can be grounded in a promissory obligation to comply with managerial directives in return for pay. It is entirely possible, in many cases, that all we have is directive power deriving from the fact that people need to make a living, and thus must do what those who have effective control of the society's productive resources tell them to do. It is entirely possible that all we have is directive power deriving from the fact that legal property rights in productive resources enable those exercising these rights to offer incentives for compliance with their directives that other people cannot reasonably be expected to resist because what is offered is necessary to live a decent life in a modern society.

It should not be thought that only societies organized around private ownership of productive property confront the problem we have been discussing. In a socialist, or state capitalist, system, where productive facilities are publicly owned, the directive power associated with ownership will often be exercised by governmental officials. But we must bear in mind the normative duality of management. Directive power is not legitimate authority. So if managers in such a system are to be understood as possessing legitimate authority as well as directive power, there will have to be a reason that is capable of justifying compliance with managerial directives when employees have moral reservations about the policies being pursued by their enterprises. It may be a feature of socialist systems, in particular, that the ability of managers to terminate employment is legally restricted in ways it is not in capitalist societies, with the result that managers in such systems possess less directive power. This fact does not obviate the need for an independent reason to comply with managerial directives that are judged morally problematic, however. If anything, it strengthens that need. When directive power of a relatively weak sort is the only thing supporting cooperative behavior, the benefits of cooperation will not be fully realized.

In the next chapter, I propose a way of understanding the authority exercised by the senior executives of large corporations in a capitalist system, which, I believe, places it on a firmer foundation. The legitimacy of managerial authority can be secured if it has the status of a subordinate form of political authority in a larger structure of such authority under ultimate governmental control.

3

LEGITIMACY: THE PUBLIC MODEL

IN THE PREVIOUS chapter, we explored the possibility of grounding managerial authority in a requirement of private morality. We supposed that in accepting employment, employees implicitly promise to comply with managerial directives in return for pay, or incur some equivalent obligation. I suggested that we understand in this way the idea that managerial authority is grounded in the consent of the employees, and I argued that it is doubtful that consent, so understood, can actually do what is required.

Some political theorists have sought to base the authority of states and governments on consent. It is often said that the authority of government is established by the consent of the governed. In one respect, this claim is unproblematic. Most people consent to being governed in the sense that they voluntarily comply with the official directives, the laws and regulations, of the polity in which they reside. But consent of this sort is simply a social fact. Where it exists, the government possesses de facto authority. If consent is to establish the legitimacy of government, it must also have normative significance. It must confer upon the government a license to issue directives. Moreover, it must work in such a way that almost all the members of a given polity can be seen as having provided the necessary authorization.

In a noteworthy book, John Simmons argues that consent lacks these features.[1] Although consent can give rise to an obligation to comply with directives, certain conditions must be satisfied for this to be the case, and the conditions are not generally satisfied in a modern state. Simmons also thinks that no other mechanism of moral obligation can establish that most members of a modern state have sufficient reason to comply with its official directives. He thus embraces a position he calls philosophical anarchism. The members of a state will have sufficient moral reason to comply with any laws directing actions that can be understood as independently required by morality—for example, laws prohibiting murder or assault. But most members of a modern state will have no moral obligation to comply with the official directives of the state as such, that is, to comply with them simply because they are the official directives of the state.

I agree that the legitimacy of political authority cannot be grounded in substantive principles of moral obligation, but I do not draw anarchist conclusions from this fact. Legitimacy can, I believe, be secured by giving political authority a different kind of normative foundation. In this chapter, I explain this possibility and argue that we can provide in the same way for the legitimacy of the authority exercised by the senior executives of large, profit-seeking corporations.

The Legitimacy of Political Authority

To repeat the argument presented in Chapter 2: a promissory obligation to comply with managerial directives in return for pay must compete with other moral considerations, especially morally important social values, that can support noncompliance, and it can be expected that some competently reasoning employees will conclude that the obligation is outweighed. This situation is made more likely because the relative weights of the applicable considerations, including considerations of moral integrity, will generally admit of reasonable disagreement. Employees who regard the obligation as outweighed will comply with managerial directives only because they need to make a living. But when a substantial number of the competently reasoning people receiving directives from some source find that only the threat of a penalty provides a reason to comply, the source cannot claim legitimate authority within the group as a whole.

71

A problem with the same structure arises in the political case as well. Many members of a modern state will judge some of the laws enacted by the government, or policies adopted by it, to be morally objectionable. Thus they may object to the state's tax and welfare policies. Some may think that the public good requires lower taxes, some that it requires higher taxes; and some may think that the existing welfare apparatus is too generous, while others may think it is too stingy. By obeying the official directives of the state, its laws and regulations, these people will be contributing, in the way described in the previous chapter, to the policies they find morally objectionable. They will be helping to maintain the state as a collective agent that pursues those policies. They will thus have a moral reason, which again could be strengthened by considerations of integrity, not to comply with the official directives of the state. Further, in the judgment of some of them, the reason not to comply may prevail against any substantive moral considerations, such as obligations of consent, supporting compliance. Members of a state who reason in this way will acknowledge no moral requirement to do what the law says simply because the law says to do it.

Governments coerce compliance with their directives by threatening punishment for failure to comply. But if a government is to be understood as possessing legitimate authority as well as directive power, there must be a justification for compliance with its directives that is independent of coercive sanctions and sufficient to support compliance by almost all the competently reasoning members of the state. One mark of such a justification is that it will secure the compliance of competent reasoners even when a failure to comply would not be detected. How might a justification with the necessary strength and reach be provided? What can establish the legitimacy of political authority?

Questions of political morality concern how political cooperation should be organized if it is to promote the public good. In Chapter 2, we saw that such questions admit of reasonable disagreement. The fully informed members of a polity, proceeding within the perspectives on the relevant reasons provided by their distinctive life experiences, will normally reach different conclusions about what the public good requires in particular cases. The relevant reasons will be provided by a set of morally important social values and a set of requirements of private morality, and the conclusions reached by a given member will constitute his or her conception of the public good. Different competently reasoning members of a polity will, then, hold different conceptions of the public good. In characterizing this divergence as reasonable disagreement, we are, in the first instance, equating reasonableness with competent operation with the relevant reasons. We can speak here of *reasonableness as competence*.

Where the members of a group that could benefit from cooperation disagree about the form their cooperation should take, the disagreement must be resolved if the cooperative benefit is to be secured. In the political case, the benefit of cooperation is the putting into effect of a sound—competently reasoned—conception of the public good. When the question of what the public good requires admits of reasonable disagreement, there will be more than one such conception. Realizing the benefits of cooperation will thus involve choosing among the contending conceptions, or generating a new one. This is one of the principal tasks of government. Government resolves reasonable disagreement about the public good by adopting laws and regulations which give expression to a particular conception of the public good. When political cooperation works as it should, this will be a competently reasoned conception. So by complying with the laws and regulations, the members of the polity will secure the benefit of political cooperation.

73

In accepting the legislative and regulatory decisions the government has made and cooperating to put them into effect, the members of the polity make concessions. They conduct their lives in a way that does not fully accord with the particular conceptions of the public good they personally hold. They thus live with a certain amount of what they perceive to be moral error. The problem of establishing the legitimacy of government is the problem of finding something that can justify the members of the polity in making these concessions.

It appears, however, that another facet of the normative notion of reasonableness can provide what we need. We have seen that reasonableness can be manifested in competent reasoning, but it can also take the form of a disposition to make concessions. A reasonable person, in a cooperative context, is a person who is disposed to make concessions to the other actual or potential cooperators, provided that they are similarly disposed to make concessions to him. We often say to people who resist concession, "Be reasonable." Similar points can be made about seeking concessions. A reasonable person will be disposed to seek concessions from the other participants in a cooperative venture when they are seeking concessions from him. We can speak here of *reasonableness in the concession sense.*

Reasonableness in the concession sense can be understood as a component of a general disposition to act cooperatively. People who are cooperatively disposed will be reasonable in this sense. It is plausible that all humans whose cognitive and motivational capacities are functioning properly will be cooperatively disposed. It follows that all humans whose cognitive and motivational capacities are functioning properly will be reasonable in the concession sense. They will be prepared to make and seek concessions in cooperative contexts when others are as well.[2] This form of reasonableness will normally be combined with the reasonableness-as-competence form. To manifest reasonableness in the concession sense, people will normally have to reason competently about what reasonableness in the concession sense requires in the situation at hand.

Fairness, too, is a matter of appropriate concession. In general, a fair way of organizing a cooperative venture—a fair cooperative scheme—is one characterized by an appropriate pattern of concessions among the cooperators. There is, then, a connection between reasonableness in the concession sense and fairness. Fairness, in the sense of fair-mindedness, is one of the main forms reasonableness in the concession sense can take. Reasoning about appropriate concession will often involve reasoning about what would be fair.[3]

Reasonableness in the concession sense can underwrite the legitimacy of political authority. We have seen that in accepting legislative and regulatory decisions the government has made, and cooperating to put them into effect, the members of the polity make concessions. They act in a way that does not fully accord with their personal conceptions of the public good. But reasonableness in the concession sense is capable of justifying the members of a polity in making these concessions. In general, reasonableness in the concession sense is capable of justifying the concessions that are necessary if a group is to realize the benefits of cooperation. In the political case, the benefit of cooperation is the organization of social life on the basis of a competently reasoned conception of the public good. So reasonableness in the concession sense can lead the members of a polity to make the concessions that are necessary to secure this result. It can lead them to conclude that they ought to defer to the decisions about the public good embodied in the laws and regulations the government has adopted. Such deference, when justified, is the mark of legitimate political authority.

This is deference in action, not judgment. It does not involve viewing the government as possessing expert knowledge of the public good. It is grounded rather in the perceived necessity of coordinating interaction to secure the benefit of political cooperation. The deference takes the form in the first instance of accepting the government's decision-making authority, its authority to decide how political cooperation will be organized. These decisions are, however, made with the expectation that the members of the polity will act to put them into effect. So the deference associated with the acceptance of political authority—the deference that reasonableness demands—includes complying with the laws and regulations the government has adopted.

This way of understanding the legitimacy of political authority is independent of promising or other forms of consent that create moral obligations. It thus avoids the problems encountered by those approaches. A government exercises legitimate authority within a polity when almost all members of the polity have sufficient, coercion-independent reason to comply with the directives it issues. And this condition is satisfied when reasonableness is capable of leading almost all members of the polity to make the concessions involved in accepting the government's decisions, and in complying with the resulting directives. The concessions involved will be concessions from each member's personal conception of the public good.[4]

I have suggested that human beings whose cognitive and motivational capacities are functioning properly will be cooperatively disposed and that reasonableness in the concession sense is an aspect of being cooperatively disposed. So when political life takes a form capable of engaging human cooperative dispositions, compliance with governmental directives can be understood as a manifestation of the proper functioning of human cognitive and motivational capacities. We can put this point by saying that under those conditions, compliance is enjoined by a requirement of practical reason grounded in the proper functioning of human cognitive and motivational capacities.

Of course, not all members of a political society will be reasonable in the concession sense. But the proper functioning of human cooperative capacities determines what reason requires in cooperative contexts. So if it is true that a given member would regard herself as having sufficient reason to comply with the directives produced by the government were her cooperative capacities functioning properly, the government can be understood as exercising legitimate authority over her.

We must be careful not to go too fast, however. It is a feature of this way of establishing the legitimacy of political authority that a given individual's compliance with the government's directives is indicated only if she can judge, when reasoning competently about what reasonableness in the concession sense requires, that she ought to accept the way political cooperation has been structured by these directives. If this is not the case—if she can competently conclude that the concessions she must make to participate in the overall cooperative project coordinated by the government exceed what can be expected of her as a reasonable person—she will face no requirement of practical reason to comply with the official directives of the state. Her only reason to comply will be provided by the threat of punishment for noncompliance.

This opens up the possibility that even the approach to legitimacy just sketched may be inadequate. Questions of political morality admit of reasonable disagreement, and this disagreement can extend to whether reasonableness requires the concessions involved in complying with the official directives of the state. As has been mentioned, it is not realistic to require, as a condition of the legitimacy of the exercise of subordinating authority within a collective agent, that every competently reasoning member be able to judge that something other than the threat of punishment provides a sufficient reason to comply with the directives in question. Eccentric reasoning can be competent. But a substantial number of members may be unable to conclude, when reasoning competently about what reasonableness requires, that they have sufficient coercion-independent reason to comply with the directives they are receiving. In a case of this sort, the claim of the source of directives to be exercising legitimate authority in the group as a whole will be called into question.

The present way of understanding political legitimacy could confront this problem. A member of a polity cannot reasonably insist on obeying only the laws she judges to be conducive to the public good. Given reasonable disagreement about the public good, if everyone demanded this concession from the other members of the polity, political cooperation organized on the basis of a particular set of laws would be impossible.[5] An individual's judgment about whether she has sufficient reason to obey the law must be grounded in an assessment of the whole scheme that the government has put in place, understood as including her prescribed contribution.

As the moral concessions she must make to comply with the official directives of the state grow larger, however, she may find that they exceed what can be expected of her as a reasonable person. As a reasonable person, she will understand that cooperation in the face of reasonable disagreement can itself be reasonable, and that concessions must be made if cooperation is to be achieved. But she will also understand that there are limits to what reasonableness in the concession sense can demand, and she may conclude that these limits have been exceeded in the case of cooperation on the basis of the government's laws and regulations. She will still respect any laws she regards as enjoining actions independently required by morality, but she will obey the law as such only because obedience is supported by coercive sanctions. If a substantial number of the members of a polity find themselves in this situation, the government's claim to be exercising legitimate authority will be open to doubt.

This threat can be reduced, however, by an appropriate choice of political decision-making procedures. Political cooperation requires that the members of a polity be prepared to make concessions from their personal understandings of how political cooperation morally ought to be organized. The decision procedure that is used to choose among the available ways of organizing political cooperation will have the effect of distributing the burden of living with perceived moral error that is unavoidable when questions of political morality admit of reasonable disagreement. In doing this, the procedure establishes the particular pattern of concessions that will find expression in legislation, but the method by which it does this can itself be assessed on grounds of reasonableness. A given political-decision procedure can be judged to be a more or less reasonable way of resolving reasonable political disagreement. It can be judged a more or less reasonable way of establishing the pattern of concessions that will find expression in legislation.

The implications for legitimacy are straightforward. When the decision procedure used to resolve reasonable political disagreement can itself be judged reasonable by the vast majority of the members of a polity, this reasonableness will transfer to the implementation of the procedure's decisions. As a result, relatively few competently reasoning members of the polity will regard as unreasonable the concessions they must make to put in place the scheme of political cooperation the procedure has selected. Relatively few will view as unreasonable the concessions involved in obeying the official directives of the state.

In modern Western polities, the procedures of liberal democracy—voting combined with civil and political rights that cannot easily be abridged by a majority vote—are widely regarded as providing a reasonable way of resolving political disagreements, and this conviction seems to be supportable by competent reasoning.[6] So it is likely that governments in these polities can claim legitimacy. The legitimacy of subordinating authority is called into question if a significant number of the recipients of the relevant directives can competently conclude that they lack sufficient reason, independent of the threat of penalties, to comply with these directives. But in modern Western polities, it seems plausible to say, this is not the case with respect to the official directives of the state.

The key point of this section bears repeating. Political cooperation among people who reasonably disagree about the public good presupposes a general willingness to live with a certain amount of perceived moral error. And reasonableness itself can demand the requisite concessions, the concessions involved in complying with the official directives of the state.[7]

The Corporate Case

In Chapter 2, we saw that the employees of a corporation can reasonably disagree about whether its actions and policies are contributing in a positive way to the public good. This in turn creates problems for any attempt to ground managerial authority in a promissory obligation to comply with directives. But on the view of legitimate political authority that I have just sketched, the raison d'être of political authority is to make possible cooperation among people who reasonably disagree about what morality requires. This suggests that we should try to apply the political model to the corporate case. Still, there is a potential obstacle to doing this.

The approach to political legitimacy presented in the previous section is not grounded in a moral obligation, which must compete against opposing moral considerations. It merely requires a member of a polity to make a judgment that the moral concessions demanded of him as a recipient of governmental directives are reasonable, where this judgment is informed by an awareness that no one can reasonably insist on moral perfection as he understands this. But the test for legitimacy remains the same. If more than a few of the members of a polity can competently conclude that the concessions demanded of them exceed what reasonableness can require, the government's claim to be exercising legitimate authority in the polity as a whole will be called into question. I suggested that if the operative political decision-making procedure can be accepted by most competently reasoning members of the polity as providing a reasonable way of resolving reasonable moral disagreement, legitimacy will normally be secured.

It may not be possible, however, to use a similar argument to establish the legitimacy of managerial authority. Suppose that a relatively large number of the employees of a corporation could, as competent reasoners, make an initial judgment that complying with managerial directives would involve concessions greater than reasonableness can demand. As an example, we might take a corporation many of whose employees regard it as fostering injustice by taking steps to prevent the unionization of the workforce. In a case of this sort, any claim by corporate executives that their authority is legitimate because the directives facilitate cooperation among employees who reasonably disagree about what morality requires will be problematic. A relatively large subset of the employees may be able to conclude that complying with the directives would require concessions that exceed what reasonableness can demand. Other corporate policies that could be regarded as morally problematic were mentioned in Chapter 2, and these examples can be multiplied.

As we have seen, in a situation of this sort, reasonable people may nevertheless be able to judge that compliance with the directives they are receiving is justified if they can view the procedure used to generate the directives as constituting a reasonable way of resolving reasonable disagreement. It was suggested that the procedures of liberal democracy have this status in Western polities. But it is unlikely, when a corporation is viewed as an independent cooperative enterprise, that the legitimacy of the subordinating authority exercised by its executives can be vindicated in this way. Decision making in a large, profit-seeking corporation is generally dictatorial. And there seems to be no way to argue that the associated procedures constitute a reasonable way of distributing the burden of living with perceived moral error that is inevitable when there is reasonable disagreement, within a group of cooperators, about the moral acceptability of the actions the group is taking or might take. So we cannot use that strategy to obtain the result that almost all the employees of a large corporation will have sufficient reason, independent of the threat of penalties, to comply with managerial directives.

Liberal democracy is not the only procedure for resolving reasonable disagreement about questions of political morality that can be judged reasonable. This decision procedure is characteristic of Western polities. But it might be possible for a reasonable member of a Western polity to conclude that the polity's decisions would better reflect competent engagement with the relevant reasons—reasons concerning what would promote the public good—if political decision making were entrusted to an elite body trained in the correct use of these reasons, a body of "moral experts." Reasonable disagreement within the polity could then be equated with disagreement within this body, and the procedures its members used to resolve their disagreements could be understood as resolving reasonable disagreement within the polity as a whole.

A position of this sort can draw support from the observation that many of the political opinions actually voiced in modern democracies are in fact unreasonable in both senses. They do not reflect competent reasoning about appropriate concession within the polity.[8] It is interesting that political decision making in the United States combines elements of both of the procedures I have described. Decisions concerning what must be done to ensure that constitutional rights are respected are made by an elite group trained in competent operation with the relevant reasons, the judiciary.

These points are of no help in establishing the legitimacy of managerial authority, however. Although the senior executives of corporations may have various forms of expertise, no one would claim that they constitute an elite trained in the correct employment of the moral considerations that bear on the public good, the morally important social values and the requirements of private morality. Consequently, the procedures that corporate executives use to resolve their internal disagreements cannot be understood as appropriate for resolving reasonable moral disagreement among the members of the corporation as a whole.

The Integrated Structure

When corporations are viewed as independent cooperative enterprises, analogous to sovereign states, the model of legitimate authority that seems to work for governments is no more successful in placing managerial authority on a secure foundation than the private model we examined in Chapter 2. But viewing corporations as independent cooperative enterprises is not the only possibility. We can instead understand each corporation as a subordinate center of cooperation in a larger, society-wide cooperative endeavor controlled by higher authority—by government. That is, we can regard the whole society as engaged in a single cooperative endeavor that has component parts.

When corporate cooperation is viewed in this way, the subordinating authority that corporate executives exercise over employees becomes a subordinate form of cooperation-facilitating authority in a larger structure of such authority in which government occupies the top place. This in turn has implications for legitimacy of managerial authority. Legitimacy depends on the satisfactory performance of this subordinate cooperation-facilitating function.

I have spoken of subordinating authority and of a subordinate form of cooperation-facilitating authority. Before proceeding, the connection between these two uses of the concept of the subordinate should be explained. If corporate executives have for any reason a license to direct the actions of employees—for example, because the employees have a promissory obligation to obey—and in addition the government has legitimate authority within the polity as a whole, there will be a sense in which, in issuing directives, the executives are exercising a subordinate form of subordinating authority. Like everyone else in the polity, the executives will be subject to the subordinating authority of the government, and thus must exercise their authority within whatever constraints are laid down by the government.

The view that I am proposing is distinguished from this by the following two features. First, the subordinating authority possessed by corporate executives is of the same kind as that possessed by the government. It is cooperation facilitating. Managerial authority is thus a subordinate form of cooperation-facilitating authority within a larger structure of such authority.

83

Second, managerial authority is a subordinate form of authority not merely in the sense that corporate executives must comply with the official directives of the state but also in a further sense. The subordinating authority possessed by corporate executives will be legitimate only if its exercise is integrated with the exercise of governmental authority in a way that creates a single, society-wide structure of cooperation-facilitating authority oriented toward the promotion of the public good.

To return to the main argument: The discussion so far has focused on the fact that corporate activities can have a negative effect on morally important social values and thus on the public good. But corporate activities can also have positive effects. Large corporations can play an important role in promoting the morally important social values. This is especially true in the case of the value of social prosperity. I characterized this earlier as the prosperity of the population as a whole. By producing goods and services for sale and providing the employment that enables members of the population to purchase these goods and services, corporations contribute to the promotion of social prosperity.

The dissident employees I have described are not impressed by such facts. They regard any morally positive results produced by their corporation as insufficient, given the negative results, to create a situation in which they are required, as reasonable people, to cooperate with the implementation of corporate policy. But when corporations have the status of subordinate centers of cooperation within a larger, integrated system under ultimate governmental control, the situation may look different. This system can be seen as having the purpose of promoting the public good—of creating or maintaining a social state of affairs that reflects an appropriate balance among all the moral considerations relevant to the structuring of political cooperation.[9] So if corporations have the status of subordinate centers of cooperation in a system of this kind, their activities will constitute component parts of a larger cooperative effort guided by government toward the promotion of the public good.

This has implications for corporate dissent. Corporate dissidents who are unable to conclude that they have sufficient reason to comply with managerial directives when their corporation functions as an independent cooperative enterprise may have a different view when it functions as a subordinate center of cooperation in a larger structure under ultimate governmental control. They will doubtless regard the total scheme of political cooperation as displaying moral shortcomings. But they may also judge these shortcomings to be of a kind that they, as reasonable people, ought to accept. A reasonable person will know that one cannot reasonably make moral perfection, as one understands this, a condition of one's participation in political cooperation.

Let's explore this idea further. A dissident employee of the sort we are considering is an employee who judges her corporation, considered as an independent collective agent, to be pursuing policies that are seriously objectionable from the moral point of view. She thus concludes that she cannot reasonably be expected to contribute to corporate cooperation by complying with managerial directives. An employee in this situation will usually comply nevertheless, but only because she needs to make a living. So for her, the executives of the corporation will possess only directive power.

If the corporation plays a subordinate role in a larger cooperative endeavor coordinated by government and aimed at promoting the public good, however, our dissident employee may be able to come to a different conclusion. She may be able to conclude that reasonableness requires participation in this larger endeavor and thus that it requires compliance with the directives that facilitate this more encompassing form of cooperation.

These directives will include those issued by the senior executives of her corporation.

It needs to be stressed that there is no guarantee that a particular corporate dissident will take this view of the matter. She may be a dissident in the larger community as well. She may conclude that participation in the overall effort coordinated by the government requires moral sacrifices on her part that she cannot, as a reasonable person, be expected to make. In that case, she will regard neither managerial authority nor political authority as legitimate. But when the operative political decision-making procedure can be seen as providing a reasonable way of resolving reasonable moral disagreement, expanding the cooperative horizon in the way that has been described will make it easier for corporate dissidents to view themselves as justified, after all, in complying with managerial directives.

We should note the role of considerations of integrity. When corporations are understood as independent cooperative enterprises, a significant number of the employees may be able to conclude that considerations of moral integrity give them a presumptive reason for dissociation. But when the cooperative horizon is expanded to encompass the overall political enterprise, the reasons of integrity for dissociation will normally be weaker. In a well-functioning polity, the larger enterprise will promote many facets of the public good, so any perceived moral flaws will not loom so large.

This argument can be strengthened by adding an observation made earlier. Whether a member of a cooperating group can regard as reasonable the moral sacrifices that participation requires will depend importantly on the decision procedures used to resolve reasonable disagreement about what the group should be doing. It is doubtful that corporate decision procedures of the normal sort can be seen as constituting a reasonable way of resolving reasonable moral disagreement among a corporation's members. But when managerial authority has the status of a subordinate form of cooperation-facilitating authority in a larger structure under ultimate governmental control, the relevant procedures are those used by the government. So it will suffice for the legitimate exercise of managerial authority that these procedures can be regarded by almost all the members of the larger society as constituting a reasonable way of resolving reasonable disagreement at the political level. It will suffice if the procedures can be regarded as constituting a reasonable way of selecting a conception of the public good to guide political cooperation generally. I have noted that the procedures of liberal democracy seem to possess this status.

Two further points should be mentioned before we proceed. First, the argument I have presented in this section does not simply validate the status quo in contemporary capitalist societies, giving employees sufficient reason to cooperate in the implementation of whatever policies corporate executives may have adopted. As we shall see, there are a number of respects in which this is so. The most important, though, is that if the legitimacy of managerial authority is to be vindicated in the way described, corporations must actually function as subordinate centers of cooperation in a larger cooperative enterprise under governmental control.

Contemporary practice in the United States often lacks this feature. Corporate executives are frequently able to influence, by means other than the presentation of moral arguments, what the government does. To the extent that this is so, corporations will not in fact possess the status of subordinate centers of cooperation, and legitimacy will be compromised. This suggests that if the conditions of managerial legitimacy that have been proposed were satisfied in the United States, many corporations would be pursuing, at the behest of the larger society, policies different in certain respects from those they are now pursuing. The situation in other capitalist countries may be similar.

There is a general point about legitimacy here. The argument concerning the legitimacy of government presented in the first section of this chapter does not have the consequence that government, everywhere and in every form, is legitimate. It rather establishes a standard that government must meet if it is to count as legitimate. The same is true of the proposal being made in this section. The claim is not that if a corporate dissident is prepared to acknowledge the legitimacy of the government under which she lives, she must also acknowledge the legitimacy of the subordinating authority exercised by the executives of her corporation; rather, it sets a standard that corporate cooperation must meet if executives are to be understood as possessing legitimate subordinating authority. The corporation must actually function as a subordinate center of cooperation in a larger structure under ultimate governmental control.

In Chapter 2, I argued that when the legitimacy of managerial authority is grounded in a promissory obligation to comply with managerial directives, there is a basis for serious doubt about whether it can be provided with a secure foundation. This is not the case when legitimacy is established in the way that is now being proposed. In a given corporation, legitimacy may be lacking because the senior executives are actively resistant to cooperation with government. But where cooperation is forthcoming, managerial authority will have as secure a foundation as governmental authority.[10]

The second point concerns quitting. I have proposed a way that employees who have moral objections to the policies pursued by their corporations may be able to regard themselves as justified, nevertheless, in complying with managerial directives. If corporate executives exercise a subordinate form of cooperation-facilitating authority in a larger structure of such authority under ultimate governmental control, the employees will be able to view compliance with managerial directives as contributing to the maintenance of the overall system of political cooperation. But it will still be permissible for employees to quit their jobs. They will have sufficient reason to comply despite their reservations, but sufficient reason to comply must be distinguished from a requirement to participate. The principle of practical reason that provides the ultimate justification for complying with managerial directives leaves each employee free to seek another, more congenial way of contributing to the overall cooperative endeavor in place in her polity—another subordinate form of cooperation that is under ultimate governmental control. Similarly, a member of a polity with a legitimate government is permitted to emigrate to a different polity whose form of life she finds more congenial, morally or in some other way.

We can now pull the strands of the argument together. It is doubtful that the legitimacy of managerial authority can be established on a private foundation. When corporate cooperation has the subordinate status described in this section, however, managerial authority will possess as secure a foundation as political authority. It will actually be a form of political authority. Corporate executives will be exercising a subordinate form of political authority in a larger structure of such authority that is under ultimate governmental control. This in turn will make corporate executives public officials of a certain kind. They will be acting on behalf of a collective agent that is oriented, in a subordinate capacity, toward the promotion of the public good.

The integrated structure of a modern society will also contain organizations that are not profit-seeking corporations. The officers of many of these organizations exercise subordinating authority over large numbers of people, and for the reasons we have explored, the legitimacy of this authority cannot be established on a private foundation. Legitimacy in these cases, too, requires that the organizations have the status of subordinate centers of cooperation in a larger structure aimed at promoting the public good.

Colleges and universities constitute an especially interesting case. They contribute to the public good by promoting the morally important social value of the advancement of knowledge. And their members, the people who are subject to organizational authority, may not share the conception of the public good that guides organizational policy. These members, however, include not only professors and noninstructional employees, who are paid for their services, but also students who normally pay something for the educations they receive. It might thus seem that in the case of a college or university, authority is exercised over the organization's customers as well as over those who serve them. But thinking of students as customers—especially if, as the saying goes, the customer is "always right"—is inimical to the educational mission of a college or university.

Corporate Democracy

In Chapter 2, I argued for the normative duality of management. This is the idea that corporate management requires two different licenses, a license to manipulate the productive property associated with the corporation and a license to issue directives to the employees. I suggested that the executives of corporations possess the former license because they are authorized to exercise corporate property rights. The standard arrangements of corporate governance in the United States allow shareholders to vote for slates of directors. Under these arrangements, then, the use that executives make of the first license they need, the license to manipulate the corporation's productive property, is subject to at least a modicum of control by nonexecutives who have rights of a kind in this property. What about the second license, the license to issue directives to employees? Is there any basis for supposing that its exercise should be subject to some sort of democratic control by employees?

In the previous section, I argued that if corporations function as subordinate centers of cooperation in a larger system under the ultimate control of a legitimate government, the license to issue directives to employees can be grounded in a requirement of practical reason. Reasonable people will understand that because issues of political morality admit of reasonable disagreement, they cannot expect political cooperation to take precisely the form they judge to be morally required. They will thus be prepared to contribute to the overall cooperative effort in place in their polity despite what they perceive as its moral flaws, especially when they can regard the decision procedure that gives shape to this effort as providing a reasonable way of resolving reasonable disagreement about the public good. It follows that reasonable employees will be prepared to comply with managerial directives if corporate executives exercise a subordinate form of cooperation-facilitating authority in a larger structure of this kind.

Subordinating authority that has a cooperation-facilitating rationale serves those over whom it is exercised by making it possible for them to secure the benefits of cooperation. Under public capitalism, the benefits of the cooperation that takes place within corporations are those of political cooperation generally, the realization of a sound conception of the public good. So the exercise of managerial authority serves the employees by coordinating their efforts, through their work, to promote the public good. Because of the role it plays in coordinating parts of the total social effort to promote the public good, there is also a sense in which managerial authority serves everyone in the polity.

To hold that cooperation-facilitating authority should be democratically exercised is to hold that it should be exercised, ultimately, by those it serves. In this section, I consider what the way of understanding managerial authority that I have proposed implies about democracy within corporations—about the role of employees in the exercise of managerial authority. Participation of the polity as a whole in corporate management is discussed later in this chapter, in the section "Two Kinds of Corporate Decision Making."

Because managerial authority serves the employees of a corporation by facilitating their cooperation to promote the public good, their autonomy as moral agents will be enhanced if the exercise of this authority is under their control. Essentially, autonomy is self-direction. As will be seen in Chapter 4, a requirement to respect the autonomy of those with whom one interacts can be understood as a component of private morality. But the value of autonomy also figures in political morality. Political arrangements respect the autonomy of the members of a polity when everyone is understood to have a right to direct his or her own actions. The contrast is with arrangements, typical of the hierarchical societies of the past, in which everyone is understood to occupy a position in an established social framework that gives the occupants of some positions a right to direct, in particular respects, the actions of those occupying other positions.[11]

When the exercise of authority facilitates cooperation among people who are autonomous in the political sense, who have a right of self-direction, respect for their autonomy requires that they themselves generate collectively the directives on which they act. In the governmental case, representative democracy, where the directives of the state are crafted by public officials selected by a vote among those who will be subject to the directives, provides the most realistic way of expressing this ideal.

This reason for democracy—the reason that it is necessary to respect the political autonomy of those receiving direction—differs from the one mentioned in the earlier sections. The earlier

reason was that democratic procedures can provide a fair or reasonable way of distributing the burden of living with perceived
moral error that is inevitable when there is reasonable disagreement about how political cooperation morally ought to be organized. Because managerial decision making resolves reasonable
moral disagreement among the members of a corporation, this
argument for democracy applies to the corporate case as well.
But the argument from autonomy is especially suited to the corporate case because the exercise of managerial authority does
not merely create rules that constrain what employees can do. It
also shapes and reshapes ongoing activity. So to the extent that
managerial decision making is democratic, employees will be
directing their own working lives. The discussion of corporate
democracy that follows will focus on the value of autonomy, but
the conclusions reached are also relevant to the argument from
fairness for democracy.

Under public capitalism, corporations are understood as subordinate centers of cooperation in a larger cooperative structure
dedicated to the promotion of the public good. But their actions
are not dictated in all particulars by higher authority. Managerial decision making plays an independent role in facilitating
cooperation among the employees. So there is a presumption
on grounds of autonomy in favor of the democratic generation
of managerial directives by employees. In its most extreme form,
this would involve the election of managers by employees.

Within an integrated structure of cooperation-facilitating authority of the sort that has been described, however, any moral
considerations that support democratic decision making apply
categorically only at the topmost level, the level of ultimate political authority. This means that ultimate political authority could
conclude that the public good would be served by allowing forms
of corporate governance in which employees have little or no
democratic control over the direction to which they are subject.

There are two important reasons why corporate governance might be given this form. First, expertise of various kinds is germane to the decisions that corporations make, and it is often appropriate for nonexperts to defer to experts (who are exercising their expertise). We saw earlier that corporate executives cannot claim moral expertise, but much managerial decision making concerns the means to be used to attain specific ends, and corporate executives may possess, or be able to draw on, expertise of this broadly technical sort. I say more about this in the section "Two Kinds of Corporate Decision Making."

The second reason concerns the role of investment in a capitalist system. Investment in a profit-seeking corporation is for the most part provided by nonemployees. Nonemployee investors are unlikely to be happy with an arrangement in which they surrender control of their investments to executives implementing the democratic will of the employees, even if it is understood that the investors have a right to the profits. But ensuring an adequate level of investment is important for the promotion of social prosperity. It makes possible the production of more goods and services and the employment of more people.

Higher political authority will thus have to weigh the presumption in favor of corporate democracy created by the value of autonomy against other moral considerations that appear to argue for a more dictatorial arrangement. But it is hard to see how higher authority could justify disregarding the presumption entirely. Devising corporate structures that give employees some role in managerial decision making—for example, mandating employee representation on boards of directors or encouraging, by appropriate legislation, the unionization of corporate workforces—will thus be appropriate in most cases.

These conclusions presuppose that corporate executives possess a subordinate form of political authority in a larger structure of such authority that is under ultimate governmental control and oriented toward the promotion of the public good. Consequently, corporate decision making is appropriately evaluated from the standpoint of the public good. It follows that corporate cooperation must be structured in a way that reflects the status of the employees as participants in a larger cooperative effort geared to the promotion of the public good. Considerations of economic efficiency, narrowly construed, provide little support for democratic participation by employees in managerial decision making. But under public capitalism, corporate cooperation is a kind of political cooperation. So the arguments that support the democratic structuring of political cooperation apply to the corporate case as well. It is noteworthy that considerations of efficiency can also be seen as arguing against political democracy, but we don't regard them as decisive in that context.[12]

The role of unions in corporate management can be understood by reference to the requirements of private morality. The contract that is produced by collective bargaining can be viewed as possessing a moral as well as a legal dimension. It can be understood as giving a particular structure to a subset of the relations of mutual reliance found within the corporation. On the private model, such relations provide the moral basis for complying with managerial directives. In negotiating the contract, a union will exert some control over the exercise of managerial authority. But if vindicating the legitimacy of managerial authority requires construing it as a subordinate form of cooperation-facilitating authority in an integrated structure under ultimate governmental control, the role of unions will be different. Management and labor will be jointly engaged in a cooperative endeavor aimed at promoting the public good. Thus unions must be understood as another vehicle in addition to, or combined with, employee representation on boards of directors, through which employees can participate democratically in the shaping of this endeavor.

Of course, under public capitalism, if employees participate in the crafting of corporate policy, they must attempt to determine what, in the light of all the relevant moral considerations, corporate policy ought to be. They must attempt to determine how the corporation can best serve the public good. They cannot simply seek to advance their personal interests.

The Nature of Corporate Subordination

Under public capitalism, the cooperation that takes place in a given corporation constitutes a component part of a larger cooperative enterprise oriented toward the promotion of the public good and under ultimate governmental control. Managerial authority thus emerges as a subordinate form of cooperation-facilitating authority in a larger structure of such authority. Subordination typically involves direction or guidance. So we need to explore in more detail the ways in which, under public capitalism, corporate executives act under the direction or guidance of higher political authority.

Business corporations have goals that are not explicitly prescribed by higher political authority. The most important of these is the making of a profit or, more fundamentally, the generation of enough revenue to remain in existence as a self-supporting financial entity. It is a central feature of capitalist societies that in the normal case, productive enterprises are responsible for their own financial viability. But by remaining in existence as entities that offer products and services for sale and that employ people to produce these products and services, profit-seeking corporations promote the morally important value of social prosperity. It is in the first instance for this reason that corporations can be regarded as contributing to the public good.

Corporations seek profit of their own accord. But the legitimacy of the authority exercised by their senior executives is grounded in the fact that these profit-seeking activities, when combined with the profit-seeking activities of other corporations in competitive markets, promote social prosperity and with it the public good. The pursuit of profit must be constrained in certain ways if social prosperity is to be effectively promoted. And because social prosperity is only one component of the public good, further constraints are necessary to ensure that it is appropriately reconciled with the other components. So the general project of promoting the public good will require the enacting of laws and regulations that shape in various ways the profit-seeking activities of corporations or that set additional goals for corporations that can conflict with the pursuit of profit.

These observations imply that under public capitalism, governmental regulation of the activities of profit-seeking corporations is the "default" option. If managerial authority is to be legitimate, the cooperation found within each corporation must constitute a component of a larger cooperative system under ultimate governmental control. Higher political authority typically gives executives a good deal of discretion in determining the precise form that corporate cooperation will take. This discretion is given to them under public capitalism; they do not have it by moral right. So when they are exercising legitimate authority, all the decisions that corporate executives make are decisions they have been authorized to make by the members of the larger polity, acting through higher political authority.

When morally private activities are at issue—for example, the conduct of family life—it is the imposition of legal regulation that requires justification. Those proposing regulation have the burden of proof. But if managerial authority is a subordinate form of cooperation-facilitating authority in a larger structure of such authority under ultimate governmental control, it is dispensing with regulation, rather than imposing it, that requires justification. Those proposing that regulation be dispensed with have the burden of proof. They must attempt to show that, in the case at hand, dispensing with regulation will promote the public good.

These attempts will normally involve the lobbying of legislators and regulatory agencies. The members of a democratic polity have a right to communicate directly with lawmakers, expressing their concerns and urging particular legislative actions. In a well-functioning polity, this communication will take the form of the presentation of arguments that succeed or fail on the basis of the soundness of the reasoning they contain concerning what would promote the public good. In actual practice, however, the reception of such arguments is often influenced by material inducements of various sorts, such as (in the United States) the provision of campaign contributions.

The question of how the resulting distortion of governmental decision making can be prevented is difficult. The problem is not usually the actual sale of a vote or a regulatory decision. Rather, the acceptance of gifts or campaign contributions creates pressure to reciprocate. Moreover, this pressure can be understood as possessing a moral dimension. In general, morality requires reciprocation for benefits received. But when legislators or other governmental officials respond to this particular moral reason for action, they fail to discharge the duties of office. And although governmental officials may be aware of this threat, the pressure to reciprocate can subtly corrupt thinking that is ostensibly about what would promote the public good.

Governmental decision making can be corrupted in this way by material inducements from interested parties of any kind. For public capitalism, however, corporate money has special significance. Under public capitalism, corporate executives have the status of subordinate public officials exercising cooperation-facilitating authority in a larger structure of such authority under ultimate governmental control. This is compatible with attempts by executives to influence legislators or regulatory agencies by means of arguments that certain policies would promote the public good. But if corporate executives are able, by making campaign contributions or by offering inducements of other kinds, to secure the acceptance of arguments that would not succeed on the basis of their logic alone, their subordinate status will be compromised. They will, in effect, be directing the government. So when corporate executives have relations of this kind with governmental decision makers, they undercut the legitimacy of the authority they exercise within their corporations.

Two Kinds of Corporate Decision Making

We can obtain a better understanding of the subordinate role of corporate executives by examining corporate decision making in more detail. We are supposing that higher political authority gives executives the discretion to make certain decisions concerning how their corporations will contribute to the overall social effort to promote the public good. There are two ways of understanding these decisions: (1) Executives can establish the means to be used to achieve ends set by higher authority, or (2) they can actually set some of the ends that are pursued by the cooperative system as a whole.

In the governmental sphere, the first function is performed by bureaucracies charged with implementing legislation. The basic function of bureaucratic decision making is to give specific form to more general objectives set by legislation.[13] To the extent that corporations confront a legislatively established framework of regulations and of incentives such as subsidies and tax breaks, the bureaucratic character of managerial authority is easy to understand. The regulations and incentives have the effect of orienting managerial decision making toward the achievement of certain goals set by higher authority. Executives then determine the precise steps their corporations will take to achieve these goals.

In a market system, however, there is another way that managerial decision making establishes the means by which an antecedently established social goal will be achieved. The market as a whole functions as a single large public institution focused on the promotion of one morally important social value: social prosperity. Social prosperity consists of the deployment of a society's resources to satisfy wants that the members of the society happen to have. Profit-seeking corporations promote prosperity by offering goods and services for sale and by converting the revenues obtained into income for their employees and investors, which enables the process to continue. No corporation aims at the promotion of social prosperity directly. But collectively the profit-seeking actions of corporations, performed in a competitive environment, promote social prosperity.

In choosing a market system, rather than a planned economy, a polity effectively establishes the promotion of social prosperity as a goal of corporate activity. So in making decisions concerning how to generate profits in a competitive environment, corporate executives determine the means that will be used to achieve a goal set by a higher authority. This gives us another respect in which the decisions made by corporate executives possess a bureaucratic character.

The authority possessed by a government is the authority to issue legally binding directives to all the residents of the territory it governs. This authority is exercised in the first instance by legislatures. But in resolving legislative requirements into more specific regulations, governmental bureaucracies also issue legally binding directives. Consequently, recent work in political philosophy has stressed the importance of creating procedures that allow affected parties to participate in bureaucratic decision making.[14] In particular, it is thought important that affected parties be given an opportunity to present decision makers with arguments supporting one or another of the options among which a decision is to be made. Thus we find governmental agencies holding public hearings prior to making their decisions.

The senior executives of corporations are not authorized by higher authority to issue legally binding directives to the population at large. But the policy decisions they make typically have consequences for various stakeholders in addition to the employees and shareholders—in particular, investors of other kinds, suppliers, customers, and members of the communities in which the corporations operate.[15] So the parallel with governmental departments or agencies suggests that corporations should establish procedures that give members of these groups an opportunity to voice their concerns and present arguments supporting one or another of the available options.

Under public capitalism, however, there is fundamentally only one stakeholder group, the members of the larger polity, taken as a whole. And the interest of this group is an interest in the promotion of the public good, to which corporations contribute as subordinate centers of cooperation in a larger structure oriented toward this goal. Particular morally important social values may be of special concern to certain subgroups in the polity, but any claims based on these values must be grounded in a judgment of what the public good as a whole requires and must be made on behalf of the larger polity. Under public capitalism, then, the activities of every corporation are of concern to everyone in the larger polity, and corporate executives can be called to account by everyone in the larger polity.

This suggests, in the first place, that any procedures that allow people affected by corporate decisions to voice their concerns should be designed so that all members of the polity can have access to them. The concerns voiced must be expressed in terms of the public good, but because issues relating to the public good admit of reasonable disagreement, the fragmentation of inputs to corporate decision making associated with stakeholder relations as traditionally understood will be preserved.[16] Of course, the members of the polity will also be able to act through the political process to secure legislation that gives the activities of corporations whatever shape they judge necessary to promote the public good. In this way, the bureaucratic authority exercised by corporate executives will ultimately be subject to the same kind of democratic control as the bureaucratic authority exercised by the heads of governmental departments or agencies.

There is, however, more to be said about relations with traditionally acknowledged stakeholders under public capitalism. In the Introduction, I suggested that in addition to the subordinating authority they exercise over employees, corporate executives exercise a broader form of social authority. Their decisions determine how the resources contributed to the corporation from the outside will find expression in corporate activity. It is appropriate to speak of authority in this connection because the suppliers of the resources defer to the judgment of the executives concerning how these resources can be used to promote the public good.

This authority is exercised over all stakeholders who supply resources to a corporation, including contributors of financing who are not shareholders. It does not normally involve the issuing of directives, but it can be understood as cooperation-facilitating. In assembling the resources that will be converted into products and services by the people over whom they exercise subordinating authority—the employees—corporate executives perform on behalf of the society as a whole an additional cooperation-facilitating function.

Extending managerial authority to encompass the suppliers of resources has the effect of expanding the boundaries of the corporation, understood as a subordinate center of cooperation to promote the public good. In some cases, this expansion could have a further aspect. Corporate executives might exercise a form of specifically subordinating authority over suppliers of resources. This suggestion is most plausible in connection with suppliers who are dependent on selling to a particular corporation. Executives of the purchasing corporation may be able to do more than use their market power to drive a hard bargain concerning the features and price of what is to be supplied. They may also be able to insist that suppliers adopt certain general policies that accord with the conception of the public good held by those executives.

Their being able to insist would be grounded in a threat of termination analogous to that confronted by employees and would thus constitute a form of directive power. Directive power of this sort can be a feature of any market transaction marked by dependence of the seller on the buyer, and it is not appropriate to speak of subordinating authority in all such cases. The justification for speaking of subordinating authority in the case of employees is that there is a continuing relationship marked by the sort of deference characteristic of authority—deference manifested in a readiness to comply, within limits, with the directives emanating from some source regardless of their specific content. The justification for speaking of subordinating authority in the case of a corporation's relations with a supplier will be stronger the more fully the relationship approximates this paradigm. If it does approximate the paradigm, legitimacy will again depend on whether the directives being issued can be understood as facilitating a subordinate form of cooperation in a larger cooperative enterprise oriented toward the promotion of the public good and under ultimate governmental control.

The status of shareholders under public capitalism requires separate discussion. Shareholders have a more direct right to participate in corporate decision making. This can be defended

on the traditional financial ground that as the "residual claim-
ants," they are more vulnerable than groups with contractually
specified claims to vagaries in managerial performance. But beyond this, the right of shareholders to participate in corporate
decision making can be understood as reflecting the fact that, to
a greater extent than other parties with a legal claim of some sort
on corporate revenue, their rights allow them to be described as
the owners of corporate property. Particularly important here
is the right to sell the company to a bidder. In general, one has
some moral responsibility for what is done with one's property
when one makes it available for use by somebody else. So it is appropriate that there be a mechanism by which shareholders can
exert some control over what senior executives do.

We can now turn to the second form that can be taken by the
decisions made by corporate executives. These decisions can set
some of the ends pursued by the overall cooperative endeavor in
place in the larger society. To put it another way, the decisions
executives make can partially determine the conception of the
public good that guides the overall system of political cooperation. Establishing the conception of the public good that will
guide political cooperation is the task of legislation. But legislative decision making can occur in subordinate centers of cooperation within the integrated structure. This will be the case when
the people setting policy for a subordinate center have been authorized by higher authority to make decisions that put in place
components of the conception of the public good that will guide
the overall social effort. In general, legislative decisions are moral
decisions that must strike a balance among all the moral considerations germane to the public good, the requirements of private
morality and the full range of morally important social values.
But decisions of this kind can be made in subordinate centers of
cooperation, and when they are, the people making them exercise legislative authority on behalf of the society as a whole.

In Chapter 1, it was noted that the decisions made by state governments in a federal system or by municipal governments within a state can be understood in this way. These governments legislate for the units they govern. The concept of the public good applies to both states and municipalities, and for the most part a state or municipal government aims to promote the public good locally understood. But there is a sense in which such governments also legislate for the nation as a whole. Where they have been given the discretion by higher authority to act as they see fit, their decisions determine in part the conception of the public good that guides the overall system of political cooperation in the larger unit. Thus because Oregon allows physician-assisted suicide, so does the United States (in that area).

Similar points can be made about corporations. When the decisions confronting the senior executives of a profit-seeking corporation require them to balance the various components of the public good, they will be exercising legislative authority within the society as a whole. Their decisions will establish a part of the conception of the public good that guides the overall cooperative effort. To take an example also discussed in Chapter 5, when the executives of media companies decide on the mix of news and entertainment that their companies will provide, they determine, in part, the way the system as a whole balances the claims of two morally important social values—the advancement of knowledge and the development of culture—against other values.

Under public capitalism, corporate executives make decisions of both kinds just described: bureaucratic and legislative. They determine the means that will be used to achieve goals set by higher authority—goals set in the first instance by the polity's choice of a market system and subsequently by the legislative and regulatory decisions made by the government. But corporate executives also make legislative decisions when they have been given the discretion to determine the understanding of the public good that will guide the parts of the overall social effort under their control. This requires the balancing of the full range of moral considerations relevant to the public good. These legislative decisions can be seen as filling in holes that higher authority has left in the overall plan for promoting the public good. Having filled in these holes, however, corporate executives must still determine the means by which the goals they have set will be achieved. So they will also be exercising bureaucratic authority. It may not always be possible to separate out these two components, the legislative and the bureaucratic, of a given managerial decision.

It is a defining feature of a democratic society that the exercise of legislative authority, which establishes the conception of the public good that will guide the overall system of social cooperation, is under the ultimate control of the citizenry as a whole. In the governmental case, democratic control is normally achieved by the election of people to office. But the members of a capitalist society do not elect the executives of the corporations the society contains. How, then, can democratic control be exerted over the exercise of legislative authority by corporate executives?[17]

In the earlier discussion of bureaucratic authority, it was noted that the society as a whole can exert control by legally mandating particular bureaucratic decisions. Similarly, it can legally mandate particular legislative decisions. Indeed, the case for doing this would appear to be stronger than the case for legally mandating bureaucratic decisions. It can be argued that bureaucratic decisions, which select the means that will be used to achieve preestablished ends, should be left to executives who possess, or can draw on, the relevant technical expertise. But no similar argument is available in the legislative case. It cannot plausibly be claimed that corporate executives possess, or can draw, on moral expertise concerning the public good. Indeed, in a democracy, there is a general reluctance to accept anyone as a moral expert to whom other members of the polity should defer because of his or her superior moral knowledge. This reluctance can be understood as connected with the fact that questions of political morality admit of reasonable disagreement.

Ultimately, the justification, under public capitalism, for giving corporate executives the discretion to make legislative decisions is provided by the fact that the polity as a whole benefits from the delegation of some legislative decision making to subordinate centers of cooperation. I say more about this in Chapter 5. When the exercise of legislative authority by corporate executives has this justification, control by the polity as a whole is achieved indirectly, through the threat that the discretion to make legislative decisions will be withdrawn—that particular corporate actions will be legally mandated—if the citizenry judges the decisions being made to be unsatisfactory from the standpoint of the public good.

This way of establishing democratic control over the legislative decision making that takes place in corporations depends on a general awareness in the larger society that corporate executives are acting in a legislative capacity for the polity as a whole. Once the legislative role played by corporate executives becomes widely appreciated, it can be expected that the decisions they make will be more closely monitored for their effect on the public good and that the withdrawal of discretion will be actively pressed by those who disagree with the decisions. This fact by itself will give the citizenry some control, as executives try to anticipate public reaction to their decisions.

The Scope of Public Capitalism

I believe that this general picture of managerial decision making is applicable to all societies where privately owned corporations seek profit in competitive markets. There are great differences among such societies in the amount of legislative discretion given to corporate executives. Higher political authority may reserve virtually all legislative decision making for itself, leaving corporate executives with only bureaucratic decisions concerning the means to be used to achieve antecedently established ends. Or it may, to varying degrees, give corporate executives the discretion to determine parts of the conception of the public good guiding the system as a whole. The forms of capitalism found in Europe, for example, seem to assign more legislative decision making to the government, while the forms found in the United States and Britain—the forms characteristic of the so-called Anglo-American model—give corporate executives greater legislative authority.

This is not the way the contrast between these two forms of capitalism is usually understood. It is usually understood as a contrast between a model in which managerial decision making is focused on increasing shareholder value and one in which executives are compelled to be more accommodating of the interests of other stakeholder groups, especially the employees. Thus in many European countries, it is more difficult to terminate employment than it is in the United States. But on the picture I have presented, in both forms of capitalism, legitimacy will require that corporate executives exercise a subordinate form of cooperation-facilitating authority in a larger structure of such authority under ultimate governmental control. So a preference for European capitalism should not be understood as a preference for an alternative to the public capitalism I have been describing. It is rather a preference for one form that public capitalism can take.

Public capitalism is a theory of the legitimacy of managerial authority and, like philosophical theories of the legitimacy of government, it is more concerned with how the possession of legitimate authority is to be understood than with the particular decisions that those exercising the authority should make. Basically, it sees corporate executives as doing what governmental officials do. Decision makers of both kinds resolve reasonable disagreement within the polity about how to interpret the public good, and about how to promote it, given the interpretation it has received.[18]

It is up to the members of each polity, acting through established political procedures, to decide which components of the total social effort to realize the public good should be placed in the hands of governmental agencies and which should be left to profit-seeking corporations. And where a component of the total effort is left to profit-seeking corporations, the members of the polity will also have to decide how tightly to constrain it with laws and regulations. Public capitalism takes no position on this. It views these questions as normally admitting of reasonable disagreement and leaves them to the political process.

It should be emphasized, finally, that for public capitalism, the ceding of legislative authority to corporate executives is an automatic consequence of dispensing with regulation. Corporate executives may not want this authority and may not want to think, in formulating corporate policy, about how it might best be exercised. But to the extent that their decisions have consequences for the promotion of morally important social values other than prosperity, they are making legislative decisions whether they want to or not. So the question of whether these decisions are being made appropriately cannot be avoided.

This point is relevant to the debate about whether corporate executives should focus single-mindedly on the maximization of profit. Under public capitalism, a single-minded focus on profit maximization will be defensible only when regulation is so extensive that all legislative decision making is taken out of corporate hands. Under these circumstances, the only decisions corporate executives will be able to make are bureaucratic decisions concerning the means by which to achieve antecedently established ends. And a single-minded focus on profit maximization, within the constraints provided by the regulations, will be defensible as a single-minded focus on contributing to the promotion of social prosperity through the market mechanism.

When regulation is less extensive, however, the decisions made by corporate executives will inevitably have legislative significance. The decisions will determine in part the conception of the public good that guides the cooperative effort in the larger society. Corporate executives must thus be prepared, in their capacity as public officials, to defend the way they have filled in the holes that have been left in the overall plan to promote the public good. It does not follow that profit-maximization must be sacrificed. As will be discussed in more detail in Chapter 5, in certain respects, profit-maximization can be combined with responsible legislative decision making. It does follow, however, that profit maximization cannot be single-minded.

Conclusion

I have distinguished legitimate managerial authority from the directive power that corporate executives possess by virtue of the fact that people need to make a living. Establishing the legitimacy of managerial authority requires identifying a normative consideration that is independent of this directive power and capable, to a point, of providing even those with moral reservations about corporate policy with sufficient reason to comply with managerial directives. I have argued that these conditions can be satisfied if corporate executives possess the status of public officials exercising a subordinate form of cooperation-facilitating authority in an integrated structure of such authority that is oriented toward the promotion of the public good and under ultimate governmental control.

4

MORALITY AND THE INVISIBLE HAND

IF THE AUTHORITY possessed by the senior execu-
tives of large, profit-seeking corporations is to be legitimate, it
must constitute a subordinate form of cooperation-facilitating
authority in a larger structure of such authority under ultimate
governmental control. In the Introduction, however, I mentioned
another respect in which corporate executives perform a public
function. Ordinary business practice in a capitalist system can
involve treating people in ways that violate requirements of private morality. In general, such actions are permissible only when
the people performing them have been licensed to do this by the
larger society. The moral phenomena explored in this short chapter can be observed anywhere in a modern capitalist economy,
but they are most socially consequential in the case of large corporations.

I have said that ordinary business practice in a capitalist system can involve treating people in ways that violate requirements of private morality. We should be clear about what this
means. The claim is not that profit-seeking businesspeople are
inevitably sucked into moral misdeeds. The claim is that the actions in question are necessary if the full economic potential of
a capitalist system is to be realized. This might be denied. Thus

the first task of this chapter is to establish that the violation of certain requirements of private morality can be a feature of ordinary business practice. We can begin with some general considerations that suggest that there can be a conflict between ordinary business practice in a capitalist system and the requirements of private morality.

Morality, Altruism, and Capitalist Business Practice

Most philosophers think that morality has some connection with promoting the interests of other people and that, as a result, morality can come into conflict with self-interest. Because to promote the interests of others is to behave altruistically, to say that there is a connection between acting as morality requires and promoting the interests of others is to say that morality has an altruistic aspect. This does not mean that morality is equivalent to altruism. Morality does not require that one dedicate one's life to helping others. Many people working for organizations like Doctors Without Borders in disadvantaged parts of the world could live more comfortably if they pursued conventional careers in Western countries, and their making the sacrifice they do is morally praiseworthy. But few would say that had they chosen conventional careers, they would have been violating a moral requirement. Although morality requires us to act in various ways to help the disadvantaged, devoting one's life to this task is usually regarded as supererogatory. How, then, should the altruistic aspect of morality be understood?

One way to see how morality can be related to, yet different from, altruism is to distinguish moral requirements from personal commitments and pursuits. As mentioned in Chapter 1, being the author of a distinctive life involves adopting personal commitments and pursuits, and the requirements of private morality can be understood as protecting the status of people as authors of distinctive lives. But the lives we craft for ourselves can differ in the amount of altruism they display. The commitments and pursuits of some people will be almost entirely self-regarding, those of others mainly altruistic. For many people, they will be partly self-regarding and partly altruistic, with much of the altruism directed toward relatives and friends. People who conform to the requirements of private morality will thus vary in the amount of altruism their lives as a whole display.

Regardless of the commitments and pursuits that have been adopted, however, respect for the requirements of private morality will introduce into all lives a basic level of altruism. Respecting these requirements sometimes involves refraining from actions that would interfere with the commitments and pursuits of others—actions that would compromise their status as authors of distinctive lives—and this is one way of promoting their interests. Further, private morality does not merely prohibit the adoption of particular ends or means of attaining ends, it also directs us to adopt certain ends that have an altruistic character. Private morality does not require that we dedicate our lives to helping the disadvantaged, but it does require that we make some efforts in this direction—that we make donations to charity, for example.

On the dimension of altruism, then, an ordinary moral life will fall between two extremes. At one extreme are egoists, whose commitments and pursuits are entirely self-regarding and who also routinely violate requirements of private morality when doing so is to their advantage—when they can get away with it. At the other extreme are people who respect the requirements of private morality and in addition have commitments and pursuits that are mainly altruistic—for example, people who go to disadvantaged parts of the world to help the people living there. Those who respect the requirements of private morality and who have purely self-regarding commitments and pursuits, or those who have a mixture of self-regarding and altruistic commitments and pursuits typical of most of us, fall somewhere in the middle.

This picture of the relation between morality, self-regard, and altruism is crude, but it will suffice for our purposes. The main point is that while merely heeding the requirements of private morality does not involve a sacrifice of self-interest as great as that associated with pure altruism, there is still a potential for conflict between these requirements and self-interest. Morality is compatible with the pursuit of self-interested ends, but acting so as to maximize self-interested satisfaction over one's whole life will almost certainly involve violating some moral requirements. In discussing the conflict between morality and self-interest, it is useful to distinguish two cases: the hypothetical case in which there is no threat of punishment for violating moral requirements and the actual case, where this threat is present and provides a self-interested reason for being moral. The conflict is less pronounced in the latter case, but morality and self-interest can still diverge substantially in ordinary life.

We can now turn to business. Although the pursuit of self-interest is to a certain extent at odds with morality, it appears to lie at the foundation of capitalist business practice. Adam Smith's claim that individuals who intend only their own gain are led "by an invisible hand" to promote the good of society is often taken as the classical expression of the foundational role in a capitalist economy of the pursuit of self-interest.[1] And the doctrine of the invisible hand has a counterpart in contemporary economics in the form of the first fundamental theorem of welfare economics. This establishes that under certain conditions, when consumers act so as to maximize utility and firms so as to maximize profit, resources are allocated to producers, and products distributed to consumers, in an efficient (Pareto optimal) way.[2] In real-world situations, the conditions are not satisfied, but the theorem still makes possible a clear and rigorous understanding of how the pursuit of private gain could have socially beneficial consequences.

Once it is noticed that the pursuit of self-interest by economic agents is fundamental to capitalist business practice, however, it is easy to see why capitalism appears morally problematic. Firms seem in some sense to be required to pursue profit, and thus the private gain of their owners or whoever has a claim to their profits, if the economic benefits of capitalism are to be realized. But because private morality has an altruistic aspect, there is a potential for conflict between the requirements of private morality and the pursuit of self-interest. So it is natural to suppose that there will also be a potential for conflict between private morality and the business practices characteristic of a capitalist system.

In Chapter 1, I noted that private morality is usually understood as containing a permission or prerogative that allows people to decline to make certain sacrifices enjoined by consequentialist moral considerations when this would require them to compromise the commitments and pursuits that make their lives meaningful. This idea figured in the argument of the earlier chapters, but it is of no help in showing that the appearance of conflict between private morality and capitalist business practice is illusory. As was mentioned earlier, the permission does not justify individuals in violating the requirements of private morality.

There is, then, some basis for supposing that capitalist business practice can conflict with the requirements of private morality. The idea that firms are to intend only their own gain admits, however, of different interpretations. If the point is that they are to pursue profit in any way they can, business and morality will indeed be at odds. But the normative import of the doctrine of the invisible hand may simply be that although firms are not to enter into transactions unless they expect financial gain, they are otherwise required to respect the full set of moral restrictions on the way people may be treated. Indeed, there is a continuum of possible interpretations of the doctrine of the invisible hand, ranging from the unrestricted pursuit of private gain, through intermediate positions in which the pursuit of private gain is partially restricted by moral requirements, to full compliance with all moral restrictions. So while reduced altruism on the part of firms may be necessary if a capitalist system is to operate efficiently, it is not clear whether this entails a lowering of moral standards as well.

The Implicit Morality of the Market

Which of these interpretations is correct? One interpretation can be ruled out immediately. The doctrine of the invisible hand cannot be understood as asserting that from the economic point of view, there should be no constraints at all on the pursuit of self-interest. The result would be a Hobbesian war of all against all, and, according to Hobbes: "In such condition, there is no place for Industry; because the fruit thereof is uncertain: and consequently no Culture of the Earth; no Navigation, nor use of the commodities that may be imported by Sea; no commodious Building; no Instruments of moving, and removing such things as require much force; no Knowledge of the face of the Earth; no account of Time; no Arts; no Letters; no Society; and which is worst of all, continuall feare, and danger of violent death; And the life of man, solitary, poore, nasty, brutish, and short."[3]

Because Hobbes is undoubtedly correct about the economic consequences of the completely unrestricted pursuit of self-interest by the members of a population, we are left with two main interpretations of the doctrine of the invisible hand. It should be understood either as envisaging a situation in which all the requirements of private morality remain in force in economic contexts, limiting the pursuit of financial gain by firms, or as envisaging a situation in which some but not all of these requirements are relaxed. But which of these interpretations should we accept? If we accept the latter, which requirements should we understand to be relaxed?

These questions can be answered by developing an account of what I call *the implicit morality of the market*. Economic agents must act in certain ways if markets are to perform their functions of allocation and distribution efficiently. The implicit morality of the market directs economic agents to perform these actions. The connection between economic efficiency and the moral value of social prosperity justifies us in speaking of morality in this connection. The model of competitive games is useful here. Part of what is required of capitalist firms if the system as a whole is to operate efficiently is the making of a consistent effort to achieve a competitive advantage, and part of what is required is respecting various constraints on these competitive efforts. One example of a constraint is the prohibition on conspiracy in restraint of trade that finds expression in antitrust legislation. A capitalist system cannot realize its full economic potential when firms conspire to fix prices.

The norms of the implicit morality of the market, then, include some that direct the seeking of competitive advantage and some that constrain these efforts. Compliance with norms of both sorts is necessary if playing the "game" is to produce the economic benefits in question. The discussion that follows is mostly concerned with the parts of the implicit morality of the market that direct economic agents to seek competitive advantage. In a recent paper, Joseph Heath provides an instructive discussion of the constraints, emphasizing their importance given that conditions of perfect competition do not obtain in the real world.[4]

The norms of the implicit morality of the market may or may not resemble the requirements of private morality, but they provide a basis for estimating the extent to which the requirements of private morality will be violated in an efficiently operating capitalist system. By comparing the implicit morality of the market with private morality, we will be able to identify (1) the cases in which the two codes require similar actions, (2) the cases in which they conflict, and (3) the cases in which some action required by private morality is neither required nor forbidden by the implicit morality of the market. This in turn will give us the components of private morality that must be respected if a capitalist system is to function efficiently, the components that must be suspended, and the components respect for which is optional from the economic point of view and thus required overall.

Fidelity to agreements may be an example of a requirement that finds a place in both codes. If agreements are not kept, only simultaneous exchanges will occur, and this may be economically inefficient. For our purposes, however, the important question concerns the possibility of *conflict* between the norms of the implicit morality of the market and the requirements of private morality. Are there such conflicts? If so, in what do they consist?

Comparing the Codes: Mutual Aid and Non-Maleficence

There appear to be at least three requirements of private morality conformity to which by economic agents would reduce the efficiency of a capitalist economy. The first is the requirement of mutual aid. This requirement can be formulated as follows. When, at modest cost to oneself, one can prevent someone facing a serious loss from suffering that loss, one must take the preventive action. It is only when the cost is modest that it is appropriate to speak of a requirement of aid. One is not morally required to enter a burning building to save someone trapped inside if there is a danger of losing one's own life. However, one must call the fire department if one encounters a situation of this sort, even though some inconvenience may be involved.

The precise actions required by mutual aid are difficult to specify. To a certain extent, it seems that what counts as a modest cost varies with the amount of good that can be done. Spending a day transporting someone to a hospital might be morally required if it resulted in the saving of a life. The inconvenience could be substantial, but if there was no sacrifice of one's major commitments and pursuits, the cost might still be modest relative to the moral gain.

Unlike the parts of private morality that rule out certain ends or means of attaining ends, the requirement of mutual aid directs the adoption of an altruistic end. So even if the efficient operation of a capitalist system requires only that altruistic ends be bracketed in economic contexts, the implicit morality of the market will still be in conflict with mutual aid. Mutual aid could, for example, require a firm to continue dealing with an uncompetitive supplier if changing suppliers would cause the old one to go out of business, with serious consequences for its employees and owners. But patronizing the supplier that offers the best price for a given product or service is necessary if the system as a whole is to function efficiently. To put it another way, what Joseph Schumpeter called "creative destruction" plays a central role in the normal operation of a capitalist system, and compliance with the requirement of mutual aid could impede this process.[5]

The second component of private morality that could interfere with the operation of the invisible hand is the requirement of non-maleficence, which stipulates that one may not intentionally inflict harm on other persons except in special circumstances.[6] This requirement appears to stand in the way of such practices as laying off employees or closing unprofitable plants in communities that depend on them.[7] But these practices are integral to the mobility of factors of production that is required for economic efficiency.

Let's look at these points in more detail. The efficient operation of a capitalist system requires the mobility of factors of production. This means that employees must be able to leave their jobs in pursuit of higher pay. But it also means that firms must be able to "leave" employees—to lay off workers, close factories, and so on—in pursuit of greater profits. These actions can, of course, have devastating effects on the individuals "left." This is why the actions appear to be at odds with the requirement of non-maleficence.

It might be argued that layoffs and plant closings can nevertheless be justified within the framework of private morality. Employment, in the United States, at least, is generally understood to be "at will."[8] Consequently, it could be thought that in accepting employment, employees consent to termination at the employer's discretion. This would be more plausible if employees had an alternative. But in any case, the termination of employment often does harm substantial enough to raise doubts about whether employees can be understood as consenting to it in a morally meaningful way. The negative effects of the termination of employment become increasingly severe the more an individual has shaped her life around a particular job. As a result, those effects may not be clearly envisaged when a job is accepted. But then it can be doubted whether in accepting employment, a given individual has consented in a morally meaningful way to their imposition.

These points can be strengthened by considering a different argument that layoffs and plant closings do not violate the requirement of non-maleficence. Many people today accept the legitimacy, as a matter of private right, of no-fault divorce, and divorce can be at least as devastating as the loss of a job one has held for many years. But the analogy is not apt. If it is permissible to end a marriage, in a case where this would impose serious personal costs on the other party, this is because the preservation of the marriage will involve a similarly heavy cost. Maintaining an employee's employment does not usually possess this feature. If a company will have to go out of business unless some employees are let go, terminating employment is morally unproblematic, all things considered. The choice is between joblessness for some and joblessness for all. Large corporations, however, often resort to layoffs when this is not actually necessary for corporate survival. The actions are taken simply to increase profits by reducing costs. Investors may welcome such actions as enhancing the value of their investments. But imposing devastating personal costs on some employees to prevent a marginal decline in the value of a diversified portfolio of investments is very different, morally, from ending a marriage one has come to find intolerable.

The routine nature of layoffs and plant closings can obscure this point, so another way of making it may be helpful. The requirement of mutual aid can be brought to bear. This provides that when, at modest cost to oneself, one can prevent somebody facing a serious loss from suffering that loss, one must take the preventive action. It follows that investors will be morally required to accept a marginal decline in the value of their portfolios so that employees will be spared the devastating personal loss associated with layoffs or plant closings. It is noteworthy in this connection that we would not be surprised to find the owner-manager of a small business making financial sacrifices to retain all of its employees during an economic downturn.[9]

The moral structure of these cases can be summed up as follows. Two parties have entered voluntarily into a relationship that creates a dependency of one party on the other, in the sense that one party will experience a serious loss if the relationship is ended. This brings ending the relationship within the scope of the requirements of non-maleficence and mutual aid. It does not follow that the relationship must be maintained at any cost to the first party, but when the costs of maintaining it are modest, private morality requires that they be borne. To put it another way, from the standpoint of private morality, entering into a relationship that creates dependency involves running a certain kind of risk, a risk that one will be morally required to make modest sacrifices of self-interest that would not otherwise be necessary. In the case of layoffs intended to increase profits by reducing costs, the relevant parties can be understood as the investors, on the one hand, and the employees whose termination would increase profits, on the other. The sacrifice required of the investors is acceptance of a modest reduction in the value of their portfolios so that the employees can keep their jobs.

But in a market system, the reallocation of factors of production in response to opportunities for financial gain is integral to economic efficiency. So we have a second respect in which adherence to a requirement of private morality can conflict with the implicit morality of the market.

Comparing the Codes: Autonomy

A further component of private morality that can be regarded as conflicting with the efficient operation of a capitalist system is the requirement to respect the autonomy of the people with whom one interacts. As mentioned in the discussion of corporate democracy in Chapter 3, the concept of autonomy finds application in political morality. There, autonomy consists in a right of self-direction, and it is respected when social arrangements accommodate this right. In private morality, by contrast, respect for autonomy plays its primary role in connection with participation in plans. To respect the autonomy of potential participants in a plan, one must ensure that they are aware of all the elements of the plan that they would regard as reasons for or against participating.[10]

Usually a plan will include some elements that the planner thinks the people whose participation she seeks would regard as favoring participation, and it will be to her advantage to make these elements known to them. So as a moral constraint on interaction, the requirement of private morality to respect autonomy mainly takes the form of a requirement to ensure that potential participants in a plan are aware of any elements that they would regard as counting against participation—as negatively impacting their interests or as morally objectionable. We can, then, understand the requirement in this way.[11]

It does not follow that an agent who wishes to involve another in a plan must describe all these elements. Some kinds of interaction have standard forms, established by convention, and as long as one's plan accords with the applicable standard form, one can assume that potential participants will be aware of many of the elements of the plan. They will be aware of this by virtue of their awareness of the conventions. For example, if one invites somebody to a birthday party, one can assume that he will know he is expected to bring a present of some kind. By contrast, if what is planned departs from the standard form, respect for autonomy requires that the details be filled in. If a "presentless" celebration of someone's birthday is planned, each invitee must be told this.

Interactions in which something is sold also have a standard form. The seller participates in the buyer's plan, but the conventions governing the sale do not require the buyer to inform the seller of the use to which the purchased item will be put. The buyer of a car need not tell the seller where she plans to drive it. This convention is compatible with respect for autonomy because the use to which a purchased item is put will normally be morally unproblematic and have no impact on the seller's interests. Consequently, knowledge of the details would have no bearing on a rational decision whether to participate in the plan. But when a buyer has reason to believe that the seller might find the intended use of the purchased item morally objectionable or might see it as having a negative impact on his interests, respect for autonomy requires that the buyer reveal these facts to the seller.

This may seem counterintuitive. Such information is rarely provided, and it may appear that a seller has no right at all to know the use to which a purchased item will be put. But intuitions can be marshaled on the other side. If Smith buys a gun from Jones with the intention of using it to kill Jones's brother, and this intention is carried out, Jones will arguably have a reason for feeling wronged that goes beyond being deprived of a brother. Had the plan been divulged, he would undoubtedly have refused to participate. So his participation was secured in a way that violated his autonomy.[12]

These observations apply to the sale of labor. There seems to be a standard form for such transactions, which provides that the buyer need not inform the seller of her full plan as long as it is not morally controversial or thought to have elements that would negatively impact the seller's interests. Thus one may hire a taxi to take one to a mall without telling the driver what one plans to do there. But if the plan is morally controversial or could negatively impact the seller's interests, he must be told the relevant details. Someone who is being hired to drive a decoy car intended to fool assassins about the location of their intended target must be informed of this.[13]

These points apply as well to employment by a corporation, which also involves the purchase of labor. In this case, however, the employer's plan is the corporate plan, or set of plans. Respect for autonomy thus seems to require that potential employees be aware of all the elements of the corporate plan that might provide reasons for or against accepting employment. The negative elements could be of either of the kinds we have been considering. Some potential employees may have moral objections to working for a particular corporation, given the policies it is pursuing. Similarly, the corporate plan could impact certain of a potential employee's interests negatively, for example, by changing the character of his neighborhood or the town in which he lives.

It is also relevant that employment has a feature that distinguishes it from the purchase of other items. The sale of most items involves alienation. All rights of ownership pass to someone else. The sale of labor cannot be regarded as involving alienation in this sense. The seller—the employee—remains attached in morally significant ways to what is sold. Thus he must be informed about any significant changes in the employer's plan that may emerge after employment begins. This point is especially germane to employment by a large corporation. Such employment is often open-ended, with no date of termination fixed at the start. Consequently, it is likely that the employer's plan will change in ways that were not anticipated initially and that engage the requirement that employees be aware of any morally controversial elements of the plan to which they are contributing, or elements that could threaten their interests.

In the case of a large corporation, satisfying the requirement that participation in a plan, or set of plans, be achieved in a way that fully respects autonomy would be difficult. Even sharing the whole corporate plan with all the employees would not necessarily satisfy the requirement. In the discussion of bureaucratic authority in Chapter 3, it was noted that technical expertise plays a large role in managerial decision making, and many employees may not be able to understand some of the technical elements— for example, concerning engineering or finance—of the corporate plan.

We can connect this fact with issues of efficiency by saying that it would be inefficient to provide all the employees of a corporation with the education necessary for full understanding of the corporate plan. But the problem goes deeper. Because of the many-faceted character of the activities of a modern corporation, participation on a basis that fully respects autonomy may not be possible. There may be no way that all employees can be fully informed, on a continuing basis, about all the respects in which the plan to which they are contributing would, or might, bear on their interests or engage their moral convictions.

If this is right, a society will have to choose between respecting the autonomy of employees and providing for the kind of economic cooperation characteristic of a modern life. An economy in which the autonomy of employees was fully respected would be able to contain only very small firms. The converse is more important, however. If the taking by firms of opportunities to grow larger can be understood as contributing to economic efficiency—by realizing economies of scale, for example—the implicit morality of the market will, simply by enjoining growth, conflict with the requirement of private morality that autonomy be respected.

It might be replied that if corporate employees explicitly consent to participation on a basis of incomplete information, their autonomy will not be compromised. So when it comes to autonomy, we can have both economic efficiency and conformity to the demands of private morality. However, just as it is doubtful that employees can be understood as consenting in a morally meaningful way to termination at the employer's discretion, so it is doubtful that they can be understood as consenting in a morally meaningful way to participation on the basis of incomplete information. The consent in question is consent to being used to serve purposes of which one is not fully aware. This can be compatible with respect for autonomy only if the people being used have a sound basis for confidence that their interests and moral concerns will in fact be respected. Such a basis may be lacking in many corporate contexts. Where it is lacking, we will not have consent that is voluntarily given. We will simply have acquiescence compelled by the need to make a living.

It appears, then, that although capitalism is not incompatible with respect for autonomy, the efficient operation of a capitalist system is. An efficiently operating capitalist system will contain large firms, and the larger a firm is, the harder it will be to ensure that the employees are aware of all the features of the corporate plan they might judge to be morally objectionable, or to threaten their interests. Moreover, this conflict between efficiency and private morality will not arise occasionally, as with the other two requirements we have considered, but will be a more or less permanent feature of a modern capitalist economy. So simply by guiding a corporation that is large, executives will be violating a requirement of private morality.

Public Morality

We have been exploring ways in which respect for the re-quirements of private morality could conflict with the implicit morality of the market, which is to say, with the achievement of economic efficiency through profit-seeking in a competitive environment. We should be clear about the force of this point. There is no inherent conflict between the profit motive and the requirements of private morality. Profit could be sought within the boundary set by the requirements. What gives rise to con-flict is that crossing the boundary is necessary for the *efficient operation* of a capitalist system. The actions required for efficient operation are specified by the implicit morality of the market, and this code conflicts in some respects with private morality.

If there is a sound moral justification for giving the implicit morality of the market precedence over the requirements of pri-vate morality, this will lie in the fact that economic efficiency is connected with the promotion of various morally important social values, most notably social prosperity, and consequently with the public good. The performance of actions that violate requirements of private morality for the sake of the public good must be licensed in some way by the society as a whole. In a soci-ety with a capitalist system, public acceptance of this economic structure as an effective means of promoting social prosperity and other morally important social values can be understood as presumptively licensing the requisite actions. To say that the actions are presumptively licensed is to say that they are licensed unless blocked by legal regulation.

128   In Chapter 1, I termed the moral framework guiding actions that promote the public good, including those in which a public service is performed by private individuals, *public morality*. But philosophers who have written about public morality have been particularly concerned with the possibility that there can be a moral justification for the violation of requirements of private morality by public officials. For example, they have discussed the use of coercion to enforce the law, which can be understood as involving the justified violation of a requirement of private morality. For the most part, however, this work has focused on violations that are unconnected with the enforcement of the law. The idea is that under certain circumstances "ruthlessness in public life," to use the title of an essay by Thomas Nagel, is morally acceptable.[14]

This claim must be carefully formulated. First, public officials must respect the law. If they are permitted to violate requirements of private morality in the course of their efforts to promote the public good, this is only because the law allows, or is silent about, some such violations. Second, the requirements of private morality do not lose their force when they conflict with morally important social values. They protect the status of individuals as authors of distinctive lives, and the preservation of this status throughout the whole population is one of the primary purposes of political association in the modern world. In general, the violation of requirements of private morality is compatible with the public good only if it makes possible a substantial gain in the realization of a morally important social value, or the prevention of a substantial loss. Third, when we think of ruthlessness in public life, we often think of political competition, the contest among individuals and groups to get their conceptions of the public good enacted into law. But the important cases for our purposes are those in which governmental officials regard it as necessary, for the promotion of the public good, to treat ordinary citizens in ways that violate requirements of private morality.

Nagel speaks, in addition to coercion, of deception, manipulation, and obstruction. Cases where governmental officials could be justified in resorting to the deception, manipulation, or obstruction of ordinary citizens are easiest to imagine in connection with foreign and defense policy. In the area of domestic policy, which is our concern here, the idea that ordinary citizens may be treated in ways that violate requirements of private morality becomes more plausible if the morally permissible treatment of individuals is understood in terms of the value of fairness. As was mentioned in Chapter 1, some of the familiar principles of private morality can be understood as identifying salient kinds of unfair treatment of individuals, which are to be avoided. But we may also find unfair treatment in situations where we cannot name any specific moral principle that has been violated. When the unfairness of an interaction is not marked by a specific principle of private morality, we often speak of what happens to the affected parties simply as undeserved.

The actions of governmental officials can involve unfairness in this sense. Thus a decision about where to build a highway or a power plant will typically result in some people losing in ways that are not deserved. But such decisions may nevertheless be justifiable as promoting the public good. These cases often have an economic aspect, but they involve more than distributive justice. They concern the way particular individuals, or groups of individuals, are treated by governmental officials. The current economic crisis provides another example. Using public funds to rescue homeowners who took out mortgages they could not afford is unfair to responsible homeowners who lived within their means and as a result have less desirable housing. But the public value of preventing neighborhood blight or of stabilizing the housing market may justify officials in facilitating such modification despite the unfairness. That these cases involve the violation of a requirement of private morality is shown by the fact that the people negatively affected react to what has happened in a way different from the way they would react to the defeat of legislation they supported. They typically *resent* the treatment they have received at the hands of governmental officials.

It is important to note that public morality also constrains the actions of governmental officials. What is usually called corruption—the necessity of bribing governmental officials to get something that one has a legal right to, or the possibility of acquiring through bribery something that one does not have a legal right to—constitutes a particularly glaring violation of the requirements of public morality. Moreover, governmental officials are prohibited from taking certain actions that are permissible in private life. For example, they may not exhibit favoritism toward relatives and friends. The actions that a governmental official takes in an official capacity must be grounded solely in the impersonal moral considerations that constitute the public good, the morally important social values and the requirements of private morality. In this respect, public morality imposes on governmental officials a rigorous standard of impartiality.[15]

We can now turn to the violation of requirements of private morality by corporate executives. Under public capitalism, corporate executives have the status of public officials. So if public officials can be understood as licensed to violate requirements of private morality for the sake of the public good, corporate executives may possess such a license as well. This will make the implicit morality of the market a component of public morality.

We have seen how respecting the norms of the implicit morality of the market, the norms directing actions that will promote economic efficiency, can involve violating three requirements of private morality: the requirement of mutual aid, the requirement of non-maleficence, and the requirement to respect the autonomy of people who participate in one's plans. These violations, too, can be understood in terms of the value of fairness. Thus the morally problematic nature of layoffs can be captured by saying that when employees have shaped their lives around their jobs, laying them off simply to increase the marginal value of other people's investments is unfair. But to the extent that layoffs increase economic efficiency, they will be dictated by the norms of the implicit morality of the market. And because of the connection between this code and the value of social prosperity, and through it the public good, the layoffs may be justified despite the unfairness involved.

Violations of the requirement to respect autonomy and of the requirement of mutual aid can also be understood as involving unfairness. It is unfair to use people in ways to which they have not fully consented. The case of mutual aid is a bit more complicated. In general, unfairness involves a failure of reciprocation of some kind. This is not always a feature of cases where aid is denied, so such denial is not always unfair. In economic contexts, however, a failure to provide aid will often presuppose a prior cooperative arrangement—it will be a failure to provide aid to those with whom one has previously cooperated—and this can give it the character of a failure to reciprocate.

The violation of these three requirements by corporate executives is just as serious, morally, as deception, manipulation, and obstruction by governmental officials. Like all violations of requirements of private morality, violations dictated by the implicit morality of the market compromise the status of individuals as authors of distinctive lives. This is shown by the fact that they typically provoke resentment. They thus require a compelling justification in terms of the public good. But because of the connection between the implicit morality of the market and the morally important value of social prosperity, a justification in terms of the public good may sometimes be available.

Earlier it was noted that public officials must adhere to a rigorous standard of impartiality. This is the price they have to pay for the moral elbow room they are granted. This may seem to present a problem for my claim that corporate executives can be understood as public officials of a certain kind. To the extent that the senior executives of large profit-seeking corporations are guided by considerations relating to private gain, it might appear that they cannot be understood as acting impartially. But closer examination reveals that this is not so.

The pursuit of private gain by governmental officials—for example, the acceptance of bribes—usually results in their failing to meet the requirement of impartiality. But when the pursuit of private gain takes place in an efficiently operating capitalist system, it will not have this consequence. If economic efficiency is to be achieved in such a system, the decisions made by firms and consumers must be determined solely by economic considerations. Buyers must seek the lowest price for an item of a given kind that they wish to purchase, and sellers must seek the highest price for an item they wish to sell. Acting in this way is thus dictated by the implicit morality of the market. But the implicit morality of the market is an impartial code of conduct. So when corporate executives adhere to the norms of this code, they can be understood as displaying the impartiality required of public officials [16]

To sum up, some sort of abridgment of the requirements of private morality appears to be unavoidable in an efficiently operating capitalist system. But it does not follow that a capitalist system is morally required to forgo efficient operation. The violation of requirements of private morality to promote morally important social values can be redeemed if it is licensed by the larger society. The precise scope of the license given to corporate executives will be determined by the legal and regulatory framework that the larger society has judged necessary for the promotion of the public good.

It bears emphasizing that under public capitalism, any violations of the requirements of private morality that are judged necessary for the promotion of the public good will be, in the end, violations by the polity as a whole, understood as a collective agent. Corporate executives are public officials exercising a subordinate form of political authority in a larger structure of such authority under ultimate governmental control. This means that they are acting on behalf of the polity as a whole. Their actions are the polity's actions. It follows that the polity cannot simply adopt the posture of a passive observer of violations of the requirements of private morality by corporate executives. It must consider whether it is prepared to license these actions as promoting the public good.

For example, the argument that layoffs dictated by the implicit morality of the market can serve the public good is an argument that they can contribute to social prosperity by freeing for other employment resources that are not being efficiently used. But in an economic downturn, there may be no place for the displaced workers to go. And it could be argued that under these conditions, layoffs do not actually contribute to social prosperity. As I explain in the next chapter, I understand social prosperity to consist in the enjoyment, by the members of a polity, of goods and services that have been produced, directly or indirectly, with the polity's own resources. This means that a polity's enjoyment of social prosperity must be seen as encompassing not just the consumption of goods and services but also the full employment of its people. If this way of understanding social prosperity is correct, the value of social prosperity might justify the restriction of layoffs in an economic downturn.

Finally, even when the violation of requirements of private morality by corporate executives can be defended as promoting the public good, this will not be the end of the matter. The polity as a whole, acting through the government, will have to consider how the moral damage done by the violations, which it has licensed, can be mitigated. This is an aspect of the larger problem, faced by any polity, of fairly distributing the costs of promoting the morally important social values. We first encountered this problem in Chapter 2, in connection with a case in which promoting environmental values would require a corporation to lay off some employees. But the problem also arises when laying off employees would promote social prosperity by increasing economic efficiency. Unemployment insurance and publicly financed retraining for displaced workers are examples of mitigating measures.

5

PUBLIC MANAGEMENT

WHAT ARE THE implications for managerial decision making of the idea that corporate executives should be understood as exercising a subordinate form of political authority in a larger structure under ultimate governmental control? What are the implications for the way executives should approach the moral problems they face? The principal implication is that corporate executives should approach these problems in a way that reflects their status as partners in a collaborative effort with government to promote the public good. If it were appropriate to understand capitalist economic activity as morally private, corporate executives could adopt a posture of guarding the private interests of the corporation's investors against encroachment by the government. But I have argued that economic activity in a capitalist system, or at least that part of it for which large corporations are responsible, cannot be accommodated within the boundaries of private morality.

Private morality cannot provide a foundation for the authority exercised by the managers of large corporations. And because large corporations are not moral persons, they do not possess the prerogative or permission that individuals acting in a private capacity possess to decline to make the sacrifices that the morally important social values can require. The activities of large corporations must therefore be understood as unfolding within the normative framework that houses the general social effort to promote the public good. Government and management become parts of a single, multifaceted cooperative enterprise, and private investment is made in anticipation of a return that can be realized under this condition.

These facts have consequences for the moral decision making done by corporate executives. Some of these consequences concern the way the collaborative relationship with government should be approached. But usually it will serve the public good to give the executives of a corporation a certain amount of discretion to decide for themselves the actions the corporation will perform and the policies it will pursue. So we also need to consider how the exercise of this discretion is affected by the fact that managerial authority is to be understood as a subordinate form of political authority. We need to consider how the status of executives as public officials structures the moral problems they have the discretion to resolve.

The study of the moral problems confronted by economic agents in a capitalist system is usually labeled "business ethics." In contemporary philosophy, business ethics has come to be understood as the general investigation of the moral dimension of economic activity, especially in capitalist systems. But the term "ethics" suggests a focus on interpersonal interactions. Consequently, the phrase "business ethics" can carry the implication that the moral problems faced by corporate executives primarily concern the way they or their employees should treat other people. If the argument I have made is correct, this idea is mistaken. Corporate executives are public officials of a certain kind, and the moral problems faced by public officials are primarily problems of political morality. They are problems concerning how to promote the public good. So the moral problems faced by

corporate executives are primarily problems of political morality as well.

Issues of political morality usually admit of reasonable disagreement. It will usually be the case that more than one position on a given issue can be supported by competent moral
reasoning. The principal social function of political argument
is to clarify what I call the zone of reasonable disagreement.
It must be borne in mind, however, that the boundaries of the
zone of reasonable disagreement surrounding a particular issue
of political morality are not fixed. Over time, the combination
of argument and social change can alter the shape of the zone.
The resolution of reasonable disagreement concerning an issue
of political morality—the choosing for implementation of one of
the positions comprising the zone of reasonable disagreement at
the time in question—will usually require an exercise of authority of some sort.

In this chapter, I do not consider any specific questions of political morality that corporate executives might confront. I do
not argue for particular answers to such questions or try to establish the zone of reasonable disagreement surrounding any.
Rather, I explore some aspects of the moral dimension of corporate management that can, I think, be illuminated by understanding the moral problems that arise in corporate contexts as
problems of political morality.

Cooperating with Government

In Chapter 3, I said that the subordinate political authority
possessed by corporate executives can be understood in either
of two ways. It can be understood as bureaucratic authority exercised in the choice of the means that will be used to achieve
goals set by higher authority. Or it can be understood as legislative authority that actually sets goals by establishing, in part,

the conception of the public good that will guide the overall co-operative effort underway in the polity. Under public capitalism, managerial authority is in the first instance bureaucratic. It is a subordinate form of cooperation-facilitating authority exercised in the choice of means to ends set by the larger society, most notably the promotion of social prosperity. Executives in large, profit-seeking corporations promote social prosperity by seeking profit in a regulated competitive environment. Profit-seeking in an environment that is suitably regulated promotes social prosperity in a way that accommodates the other components of the public good, the other morally important social values and the requirements of private morality.

As I understand the value of social prosperity, it consists of the enjoyment by the members of a polity of goods and services they want to have when they themselves have produced these goods and services. The promotion of social prosperity is compatible with international trade. In international trade, local wants are satisfied in part by the use of foreign resources. But the process is reciprocal. Local resources are used to satisfy foreign wants, earning a return that can be spent locally. So by an indirect route, local wants are satisfied by local productive activity. Goods and services provided in the form of aid from outside the polity, by contrast, do not increase its prosperity. And although the provision of aid by some members of a polity to other members does not diminish the prosperity of the polity as a whole, the fact that some people require aid can be an indication that prosperity is not as great as it might be.

The value of social prosperity is tied, then, to the efficient use of the available resources, including human resources, to satisfy wants the members of the polity in question have for goods and services. It should also be mentioned that the prosperity of a polity will have a history, not just in the sense that the available resources will increase or diminish but also in the sense that the wants that are satisfied will change. One important reason for this, especially in a polity that relies on profit-seeking firms to promote prosperity, is that new products and services will be developed that many people come to want. Recent examples in the United States include flat-screen TVs and exotic coffee drinks.

A polity with a market system may still experience market failure of various sorts. Clean air provides an example. Much production creates air pollution, and when this is taken into account, the cost to the polity of producing particular items may exceed the benefit. The purchasers benefit from the items, but the price they pay does not reflect the full social cost of production. In more technical terms, external diseconomies of production are associated with processes that create pollution. The usual remedy is the legislative mandating, and the bureaucratic specification, of measures that have the effect of internalizing costs so that consumers pay the full social cost of producing the things they want. Thus a government might mandate the installation of pollution control equipment in power plants, with the cost being passed on to the users of the electricity.

Regulation that reduces air pollution can be understood as promoting social prosperity. People generally want clean air. But usually such regulation will promote other morally important social values as well. Thus the curbing of air pollution promotes the morally important social values of the preservation of the environment and the maintenance of the health of the population. This means there are reasons for such regulation that are independent of the fact that people happen to want clean air. The point can be put by saying that if the members of a polity did not happen to want clean air, there would still be moral reasons for them to take the steps necessary to produce it.

A parallel with the case of an individual may make this idea clearer. It is possible to understand human well-being in terms of want satisfaction. A good life for a human being will then be one in which her wants are fully, or mostly, satisfied. But this view is inadequate. A good human life must possess features that are independent of the satisfaction of the wants the individual in question simply happens to have. Thus a life that lacks accomplishment, autonomy, understanding, or deep personal relationships will be missing something, even if the particular wants the individual in question happens to have are fully satisfied. Conversely, living a life that contains these features may involve accepting less want satisfaction overall. John Stuart Mill makes an analogous point when he says, "It is better to be a human being dissatisfied than a pig satisfied, better to be Socrates dissatisfied than a fool satisfied."[1]

The well-being of a polity can be understood similarly. I have said that the morally important social values correspond to certain forms of aggregate well-being in a population. It may be useful to repeat the list here. They include, in addition to social prosperity, distributive justice, the rule of law, national defense, the preservation of the environment (to the extent that it affects human welfare), the maintenance of the health of the population, the advancement of knowledge (understood broadly as encompassing the creation of an educated and informed populace), the fostering of community, and the development of culture. Promoting social prosperity involves satisfying wants that the members of a polity happen to have. But a polity that lacks the forms of aggregate well-being identified by the other morally important social values, or in which these forms of well-being are inadequately realized, cannot be doing well as a polity, even if the particular wants its members actually have are well satisfied. And bringing into existence these other forms of aggregate well-being may require the members of the polity to accept a somewhat lower overall level of want satisfaction.

It follows from these observations that the promotion of social prosperity can conflict with the promotion of other morally important social values. The efficient use of a polity's resources to satisfy wants its members actually have may fail to serve the public good because people fail to want some of the things that are required for social well-being or because they have wants the satisfaction of which interferes with the provision of these things. When this is the case, economic activity must be regu- **141** lated, or supplemented with governmental action, not only to correct market failure that threatens the promotion of social prosperity but also to ensure the promotion of these other components of the public good.

In a democratic polity, adopting such steps requires general acceptance of the idea that all the morally important social values provide reasons relevant to the organization of political cooperation. The same is true of the requirements of private morality, since respect for them also promotes the public good. Because questions of political morality admit of reasonable disagreement, a consensus on what all these considerations, taken together, require is not to be expected. But democratic procedures provide a way of resolving such disagreements.

I discuss these matters further in the next section. Here I want to focus on what the points just made imply for relations between corporate management and government. In particular, I want to focus on what they imply about the proper role of corporate management in the political process that establishes the laws and regulations to which economic activity will be subject. This was discussed in Chapter 3, but more should be said.

Public management is management from the standpoint of the system as a whole. Corporate executives can legitimately seek profit within a regulatory framework designed to ensure that the system as a whole promotes the public good. In so doing, they will be acting to promote social prosperity in a way that accommodates the claims of the other components of the public good, as determined by the larger political process. But they cannot legitimately attempt to change the regulatory framework simply to secure greater profit for their corporations. A corporation's pursuit of profit in competitive markets has a place in public capitalism as a means of promoting social prosperity and thus the public good. But a corporation's pursuit of profit as an end in itself does not. So any efforts to secure changes in the regulatory framework must be justified on the ground that the changes will contribute in a desirable way to the public good.

In fact, the arguments that corporate executives make when they seek to participate in the political process are usually formulated in this way. They often claim that the creation, maintenance, or elimination of certain regulations will promote the public good. But the problem of rationalization looms large. Corporate executives typically do not attempt, through deliberative exchange with the other members of the polity, to determine what would best serve the public good. And often their arguments merely provide conceptual clothing for an effort to advance the interests of the corporation as a profit-seeking entity.[2]

On the view taken in this book, issues of political morality admit of reasonable disagreement. The unique experiences of the members of a polity can give them distinctive perspectives on the requirements of political morality that the available concepts enable them to articulate. And these perspectives can be correct, in the sense that they reflect competent moral reasoning carried out within the framework of those experiences, even though other people reasoning competently can reach different conclusions. John Rawls attributes reasonable disagreement to certain burdens of judgment, one of which he characterizes as follows: "To some extent (how great we cannot tell) the way we assess evidence and weigh moral and political values is shaped by our total experience, our whole course of life up to now, and our total experiences must always differ. Thus in a modern society with its numerous offices and positions, its various divisions of labor, its many social groups and their ethnic variety, citizens' total experiences are disparate enough for their judgments to diverge, at least to some degree, on many if not most cases of any significant complexity."[3]

But as was discussed in Chapter 2, reasonable disagreement must be distinguished from the distribution of opinion we find when people are simply rationalizing private interests. We can usually be confident that a difference of opinion represents reasonable disagreement when it survives reasoned debate carried out in good faith over an extended period of time. But many disagreements concerning the regulation of economic activity do not give rise to reasoned debate carried out in good faith. Thus it will often be unclear whether the positions taken are reasonable. A position that would serve the interests of the person taking it may be one that could be supported by competent reasoning carried out within the framework of her experiences. But when people are defending political positions that also accord with their interests, rationalization is always a possibility.

We also need to bear in mind that participation in genuinely shared deliberation must be distinguished from mere advocacy. Contributions to political discourse are often explicit attempts to make a case, in the court of public opinion, for one party to a dispute. The goal is to defeat opposing arguments. Genuinely shared deliberation, by contrast, involves a readiness on the part of the participants to modify or abandon their positions if the opposing arguments, considered with an open mind, require this. The zone of reasonable disagreement concerning a particular issue of political morality consists of the set of positions on that issue that would remain after genuinely shared deliberation.

To summarize, when corporate executives are understood as exercising a subordinate form of cooperation-facilitating authority in a larger structure under ultimate governmental control, their goal in participating in the larger political process that determines the legal framework within which economic activity will unfold cannot be to advance the interests of their corporation or the people who have invested in it. It must rather be to join the general public discussion about how economic activity can best serve the public good. Discharging this role in good faith requires an awareness of the distinction between genuine moral deliberation, on the one hand, and rationalization, or advocacy, on the other.

The Legislative Authority of Management

Market failure often involves a failure to produce public goods. Simply put, these are goods that cannot be provided to anyone in a particular group without being provided to everyone. More accurately, public goods are characterized by nonrival consumption (consumption by one person does not reduce the opportunity of others to consume) and nonexcludable consumption (no one in the relevant group can be excluded from consumption). Public goods must not be confused with *the* public good, the appropriate reconciliation of all the moral considerations relevant to the organization of political cooperation. Clean air is a public good. It cannot be provided to anyone in the relevant region without being provided to everyone. Another example is a listener-supported radio station, which is a public good (for anyone with a radio) within broadcast range.

The promotion of social prosperity, defined as the conversion of a society's resources into goods and services that its members want, requires the provision of public as well as private goods. Some of the things that the members of a society want will be things that cannot be provided to any of them without being provided to all. Also important are goods that are not public in the technical sense described in the previous paragraph but are usually publicly available once they have been provided, such as roads, railroad stations, and airports. Normally, rational action by consumers and firms interacting in a market is not capable of securing the provision of public goods or goods of this second, publicly available sort. The fact that people can consume the good without paying for it renders market provision impossible. The members of the group that would benefit from the production of such a good must act collectively to produce or purchase it. This can be done privately, as in the case of a listener-sponsored radio station. But in the most important cases, the collective production or purchase of goods of these kinds is effected by governmental action. Thus a government might mandate steps designed to reduce air pollution or to build a road.

These points about market failure and public goods show that even the promotion of social prosperity cannot be entrusted entirely to markets. But it does not follow that the role of profit-seeking corporations in the overall social effort to promote the public good is restricted to the provision of the particular components of social prosperity that can be left to markets. There will normally be some overlap between social prosperity and other morally important social values. This was noted in the previous section in connection with the public good of clean air. Reducing air pollution usually means that a population's resources are being used more efficiently to satisfy its wants. But the reduction of air pollution will promote the morally important social values of the preservation of the environment and the maintenance of the health of the population as well.

This kind of overlap among morally important social values can also be found in connection with the specifically profit-seeking activities of corporations. Promoting morally important social values other than prosperity involves, among other things, providing congenial living environments, preserving or restoring people's health, keeping people informed about matters of public concern, and providing cultural products to people. The profit-seeking activities of corporations can have these effects. The promotion of social prosperity by efficient markets involves the provision of goods and services that the members of a polity want and are willing to pay for. Although social prosperity is a moral value, the goods and services the consumption of which contributes to social prosperity need not possess any moral value. To take one example, the production and consumption of cookies has no independent moral value.[4] But congenial environments, healthy lives, information about public affairs, and cultural offerings do possess independent moral value. Their production and consumption contributes by itself to the aggregate well-being of a polity. And they are among the things that people want and are willing to pay for. So to the extent that profit-seeking firms service this demand, the promotion of social prosperity by market mechanisms will involve the promotion of other morally important social values as well.

As we saw in the previous section, in ascribing moral importance to these other values, we are supposing that the claim they have on us does not depend on what people simply happen to want. If maintaining the health of the population has moral importance in its own right, a society will have a reason to take steps to maintain the health of the population even if this means that the overall level of want satisfaction is reduced. In some respects, a society's choice of a market system reflects confidence that few sacrifices of this sort will be necessary. When the promotion of values other than social prosperity requires the provision of public goods, or the publicly available goods mentioned earlier, market activity will have to be supplemented by collective action. But otherwise, according to this view, profit-seeking activities will do justice to the full range of morally important social values.

Under current conditions, however, this is not realistic. The problem is especially pronounced in profit-seeking corporations that can be regarded as having the social function of promoting particular moral values other than prosperity. Thus media companies can be regarded as having the social function of promoting the advancement of knowledge and the development of culture. But the imperative to maximize profit may drive their executives to provide less news and more mindless entertainment. Similarly, pharmaceutical companies have the social function, along with other companies operating in the healthcare sector, of maintaining the health of the population. But the profit motive may lead their executives to under- or overproduce certain medicines, or to price them in a way that makes them inaccessible to some who need them, thus compromising the health of the population as a whole. Analogous points can be made about medical insurance companies. Considerations of profit maximization can lead their executives to adopt practices that have the effect of denying members of the population necessary care, again compromising the health of the population as a whole.

A polity can respond to this problem in any of several ways. It can take the promotion of certain morally important social values out of the hands of the market, entirely or partly, as is done in Britain with the National Health Service and the BBC. Alternatively, it can enact legislation designed to force corporations to pursue policies that are more accommodating of values other than social prosperity. This will mean legally requiring corporations to forgo some courses of action that could result in greater profits. Thus, medical insurance companies might be prevented from dropping policyholders who find themselves with serious diseases. When the same requirements are imposed on all the firms in a given industry, no firm will be placed at a competitive disadvantage.

It is often thought, however, that the decentralized decision making characteristic of a market system has social benefits.

So we should consider the possibility that corporate executives, acting independently, might be able to modify the profit-seeking activities they direct so as to accommodate the demands of morally important social values other than social prosperity. This presupposes that the regulatory framework provides the space for such actions.

In making decisions of this kind, corporate executives would be exercising legislative, in contrast to bureaucratic, authority. They would not simply be selecting the means to be used to achieve ends established by higher authority. They would be setting some of the ends pursued by the overall system of political cooperation. They would be making judgments that determine, in part, the conception of the public good that guides the overall cooperative effort in the polity—judgments that determine, in part, how values such as the advancement of knowledge, the development of culture, and the maintenance of the health of the population will be promoted by the system as a whole. To use the image employed in Chapter 3, they would be filling in holes that governmental decision making has left in the overall plan for promoting the public good. In ceding this legislative authority to corporate executives, a polity will, in a further respect, be conferring upon them the status of public officials.

As mentioned in Chapter 3, if the regulatory framework gives corporate executives the discretion to make these decisions, they cannot avoid exercising it. If they decide to focus single-mindedly on the pursuit of profit, defending this, when challenged, by saying that their corporations can promote the public good most effectively in this manner, they will still be making a legislative decision for the society as a whole.[5] When corporate executives make that particular legislative decision, they create a situation in which the larger society is forced to resort to regulation, or nonmarket mechanisms, to promote the full set of morally important social values. But can corporate executives be expected to take any other course of action? Can they be expected to do anything but focus single-mindedly on the pursuit of profit?

It is a fundamental feature of a capitalist system that firms are responsible for their own financial viability and must seek to maintain it in a competitive environment. It is worth mentioning that socialist systems must also be concerned with financial viability. Although some productive activities can be subsidized, it will not be possible to subsidize them all. It will not be possible—long term, given that loans must be repaid—for the society as a whole to consume more than it produces. From the standpoint of financial viability, the difference between capitalism and socialism is that under capitalism, the task of securing the financial viability of the society as a whole is delegated to independent productive enterprises, which are responsible for their own financial viability.

This has consequences for the promotion of the public good in a polity with a capitalist system. The need to maintain the financial viability of the corporation limits the steps that executives can independently take to promote morally important social values other than prosperity. If people want to watch television shows that feature mindless entertainment, an unsubsidized network that offers a great deal of news and public-affairs programming, together with serious cultural offerings, will have difficulty surviving. Similarly, a pharmaceutical company that decides what medicines to produce solely by determining what will contribute to the health of the population, taking no account of whether there will be enough demand to cover the costs of development and production, will have difficulty surviving.

A capitalist society must, then, be prepared to constrain or supplement market activity in various ways if the public good as a whole is to be successfully promoted. This is not a flaw in capitalist systems. It is simply a consequence of the fact that profit-seeking that conforms to the implicit morality of the market directly promotes only one of several different morally important social values, the value of social prosperity. The fact that profit-seeking in competitive markets promotes this central value automatically is a great virtue of capitalist systems. But it is a mistake to look for a similarly automatic promotion of the other social values. Their promotion will require deliberate steps on the part of the society.

These deliberate steps can, however, be taken by the executives of profit-seeking corporations. The exercise of legislative authority by corporate executives—that is, their making decisions that orient their corporations toward the promotion of morally important social values other than social prosperity—would have beneficial consequences if it could be made to work. The decentralized decision-making characteristic of market systems allows a wide range of social experimentation, which is desirable when decisions balancing the claims of different morally important social values are required. A federal system of political authority provides this benefit. Policies that succeed in one state or province can be copied in others. And further benefits of this sort could be achieved if legislative decision making that was genuinely responsive to values other than social prosperity could take place in corporations as well.

The key to this possibility lies in the interpretation of the idea that profit-seeking activities must be modified to accommodate the claims of other morally important social values. If "modified" means "curbed," so that the pursuit of profit is sacrificed to other goals, there will be severe constraints on the ability of corporate executives to respond, independently of regulation, to the claims of morally important social values other than prosperity. But this is not the only way of understanding the modification of profit-seeking so as to accommodate values other than prosperity. Executives can instead seek to identify ways of *combining* the pursuit of profit with the promotion of other morally important social values. They would then be focusing on the pursuit of profit, but they would not be pursuing it single-mindedly.

We can begin to get an idea of what is involved here by considering how the promotion of the value of social prosperity itself can take on a legislative, in contrast to a bureaucratic, character. In the previous section, I mentioned that social prosperity has a history, in the sense that new products and services are developed that many people come to want. I gave as examples flat-screen TVs and exotic coffee drinks. On the view I have been describing, social prosperity is one component of the public good, so by changing the way it is interpreted such developments change the way the public good as a whole is understood. The widespread possession of flat-screen TVs or consumption of exotic coffee drinks could come to be regarded as a salient manifestation of a society's prosperity, with consequences for how people think about the public good. Also worth mentioning here are changes in the way goods and services are marketed. The development of online auction sites like eBay, for example, has altered the way social prosperity is promoted, with consequences for the way the public good is understood. Changes in the interpretation of social prosperity are often a result of the efforts of entrepreneurs, so within the framework of public capitalism entrepreneurial activity can possess a legislative character. Such activity takes place both inside and outside established corporations.

Innovation of the kind just described changes the way the public good is understood by changing the way social prosperity is interpreted. But there is no reason why such innovation cannot at the same time promote other morally important social values. We have seen that the promotion of social prosperity can overlap with the promotion of other morally important social values because people want, and are willing to pay for, items the provision of which promotes these values—for example, information about public affairs.

The overlap is not complete, which is why a society with a capitalist system must be prepared to supplement profit-seeking in competitive markets with governmental action that creates goods the market cannot or will not provide and that shapes market activity in socially desirable directions. But although the overlap is not complete, the area within which profit-seeking in competitive markets can at the same time promote other morally important social values is not fixed. Innovative thinking by the members of corporations can identify new ways of bringing the promotion of moral values other than prosperity within the scope of market activity. That is, profit-seeking corporations can develop new products and services for which people are willing to pay, yet which have the feature that their provision and consumption promotes other morally important social values as well.

Like executives of companies whose products merely change what people want, executives of the companies we are now considering will be altering how social prosperity is interpreted. But because the new interpretation will increase the overlap with other morally important social values, the innovations will have legislative significance of a further sort. They will orient social cooperation generally toward the promotion of values other than prosperity, in this way filling in gaps that governmental decision making has left in the conception of the public good that guides social cooperation. Some recent corporate decisions that can be seen as expanding the overlap between social prosperity and other morally important social values are those leading to the development and marketing of personal computers and smart phones. The production and purchase of these items has promoted the advancement of knowledge as well as social prosperity. Another example is the development of electric cars, the production and purchase of which promotes environmental values as well as social prosperity. And companies developing new technologies for the medical field can be seen as expanding the overlap between social prosperity and the maintenance of the health of the population.

I said earlier that legislative decision making that orients corporate activity toward morally important social values other than prosperity would have beneficial consequences if it could **153** be made to work because it would allow experimentation in the overall social effort to promote the public good. We should be clear about what is involved in making it work. When profitability is the sole goal, corporate executives simply need to find out what people want, or can be brought to want, and give it to them. For the sort of corporate legislation we are now considering, more is required. Like the regulation of business or the creation of governmental agencies charged with promoting specific morally important social values, the development of products and services that can be sold at a profit, but whose consumption will promote values other than social prosperity, must be guided by a conception of the public good. Corporate executives will have to think creatively about what would serve the public good in all its dimensions. They will have to identify ways that certain morally important social values are not being effectively promoted by the overall system of social cooperation and then initiate efforts to develop products or services that will address these deficiencies while also generating a profit for the corporation. In short, under public capitalism, the responsible exercise of legislative authority by corporate executives will require that they think like the public officials they are.

Similar points can be made about consumers. In the cases we are discussing, the promotion of social prosperity overlaps with the promotion of other morally important social values. This means that legislative decisions by corporate executives could achieve their goals even if consumers made purchases the normal way, without considering the significance of their decisions for the public good. But if the moral potential of corporate legislation is to be fully realized, consumers must be prepared to think constructively about how their purchasing decisions can contribute to the public good. It is unrealistic to expect more than a few consumers to make purchases that are judged inferior from the standpoint of want satisfaction simply because consuming the items in question will promote a morally important social value other than prosperity. But with a little reflection, consumers may come to see that an item of this sort that initially appeared unacceptable from the standpoint of want satisfaction would actually be quite acceptable. That is, reflection on the part of consumers provides a further way that a society's wants can evolve, increasing the overlap between social prosperity and other morally important social values.

Under public capitalism, executives must convince the larger society that their legislative decisions deserve support in the form of purchasing decisions. This means that responsible legislative decision making by corporate executives will have to involve a dialogue with consumers that transcends the mere offer of a product or service at a certain price, or bargaining over price. Executives will have to explain to consumers the legislative decisions they have made, or are contemplating making, and receive feedback from them. Genuine dialogue of this sort will involve shared deliberation, so the image advertising that corporations now provide cannot be understood as a contribution to it. The Internet has greatly expanded the possibilities for dialogue between corporations and the wider public.

In presenting the theory of public capitalism, I have made the assumption that questions of political morality admit of reasonable disagreement. Legislative decision making by corporate executives will affect the evolution of the zone, or zones, of reasonable disagreement in a polity. Normally, the question of whether a new product contributes to the promotion of a morally important social value other than prosperity, or if it does, whether the overall result is an improvement from the standpoint of the public good, will admit of reasonable disagreement. For example, some might question whether the development and widespread use of smart phones contributes enough to the advancement of knowledge to counterbalance the negative consequences for this and other social values of the tethering of people to these devices. It might be thought that the development of the devices has created a situation in which the receipt of information takes up so much time that there is little left for digesting it and reflecting on its larger significance.

But the members of the society, through their purchasing decisions, will be supporting one or the other of the positions that can be taken on such an issue. When a polity uses an institutionalized decision procedure like voting to resolve reasonable disagreement about the public good, it comes down definitively on one side or the other,. But when reasonable disagreement concerns the consequences for the public good of the production and consumption of items that can be purchased in a market, people on both sides of the issue can give their views social effect. Those who regard the emergence of a particular product or service as a positive development from the standpoint of the public good can support it with purchasing decisions, while those who don't can refrain. If a product or service contributing to the promotion of a social value other than prosperity is embraced by a large part of the population, however, the resulting change in the social environment may precipitate changes of mind by people who were initially unconvinced. Skeptics about smart phones may be won over as their use becomes more widespread. In this way, legislative decisions made by corporate executives can contribute to what I call the *conceptual-cum-social process* through which competent reasoning about the public good—and with it, the zone of reasonable disagreement—evolves over time.[6]

We have been envisaging legislative decision making by corporate executives, their making decisions that establish, in part, the ends the overall system of social cooperation will be promoting, and thus the conception of the public good that will guide the overall system. In Chapter 3, it was noted that although corporate executives normally possess, or can draw on, the technical expertise required for sound bureaucratic decision making, they have no particular moral expertise. They cannot be understood as experts on the public good. Nevertheless, when higher political authority makes possible dictatorial decision making by corporate executives, it authorizes executives to exercise their own judgment about how to respond to moral considerations other than social prosperity.

This may seem problematic. Precisely because decisions about what would promote the public good cannot be entrusted to experts, the case for the democratic exercise of legislative authority is stronger than the case for the democratic exercise of bureaucratic authority. But legislative decisions of the sort we have been considering will have a significant social impact only if they are supported by purchasing decisions. And as has been mentioned, purchasing decisions can be grounded in shared deliberation about the public good, with the result that corporate legislation is controlled by a wider range of moral judgment. Also, the legislative decision making in the economic sphere envisaged by public capitalism is accomplished in a decentralized way. So the overall impact of a given legislative decision will usually be smaller than if a decision with the same content had been made by a government, initially at least. Consequently, the larger society will have time to assess the impact that a particular piece of corporate legislation is having on the public good.

To summarize, promoting the public good requires doing more than satisfying, through productive activity, the wants the members of a polity simply happen to have. It requires the promotion of morally important social values other than social prosperity. Thus political cooperation must be organized accordingly. This can be done by leaving the promotion of social prosperity to profit-seeking corporations while resorting to governmental action to promote the other values. But when the regulatory framework gives corporate executives choices about the extent to which, or the way in which, the activities they control will contribute to morally important social values other than social prosperity, the making of these choices inevitably involves the exercise of legislative authority. The decisions that are made will establish, in part, the conception of the public good that guides the system as a whole. In a competitive environment, it will be difficult for executives to sacrifice, to any significant degree, the pursuit of profit. But as we have seen, the pursuit of profit can be combined with the promotion of other morally important social values. When this is the case, the promotion of these other values can be accomplished, up to a point, without direct governmental action.

It must be borne in mind that under public capitalism the legislative authority that corporate executives possess is delegated to them by the larger society. So if it is not exercised responsibly by a particular corporation, or if the overall effort in the corporate sector starts to display a certain incoherence from the standpoint of the public good, the larger society can take the legislative decisions in question out of corporate hands, either by imposing regulations or by establishing governmental agencies charged with promoting the public good in the respects at issue. The threat of such action will give corporate executives an incentive to take their legislative responsibilities seriously.

Mergers and Acquisitions

So far, we have been discussing some features of the moral dimension of the management of a single corporation. One of the most noteworthy facts about modern capitalist societies, however, is that corporations, understood as social entities of a certain sort, undergo fission and fusion. A given corporation may split apart, often as a result of the sale of a component to another corporation, or it may merge with another corporation to form a larger entity. Mergers, too, often involve sale. The merger is a result of the purchase of one corporation by another. The political theory that I have presented makes a distinction between legitimate authority and directive power. Mergers and acquisitions alter the relations of directive power to which employees, and perhaps others, are subject. Directive power is wielded, especially at the topmost levels, by a different group of individuals, but directive power is not legitimate authority. So we need to consider how mergers and acquisitions affect the legitimacy of managerial authority.

We can pose this question by imagining a corporation whose executives constitute legitimate authorities of the sort I have described. They exercise a subordinate form of cooperation-facilitating authority in a larger structure that is under ultimate governmental control. By the argument of Chapter 3, the employees of the corporation thus have sufficient reason, within limits, to comply with managerial directives even when they regard these directives as morally mistaken. If the corporation merges with another corporation, will its employees continue to have this reason to comply with managerial directives, or will legitimacy be lost?

Mergers and acquisitions are property transactions. In the simple case involving two corporations, the productive property of one corporation is merged with that of another. The parties to the transaction are the owners. The owners of the two corporations often become joint owners of the new, merged entity. In a publicly held corporation, the owners, in the sense relevant to mergers and acquisitions, are the shareholders, so they must ultimately approve the deal. Mergers and acquisitions are typically initiated by the senior executives of one of the corporations, which is to say, top management and the board of directors. Such overtures may receive a friendly reception from the senior executives of the other corporation, in which case both management teams will seek the agreement of their respective shareholders. Alternatively, one team may attempt a hostile takeover by appealing to the shareholders of the target corporation over the heads of the senior executives. In the case of a hostile takeover, resistance to the proposed merger or acquisition on the part of the senior executives of the target corporation is usually grounded in the expectation that the new regime will put them at a disadvantage. This can be true for the employees as well, because mergers and acquisitions typically result in layoffs. For this reason, the employees may support resistance.

The legitimacy of managerial authority, as I have characterized it, can be preserved through mergers and acquisitions. The legitimacy of managerial authority is grounded in the fact that corporate executives are exercising a subordinate form of cooperation-facilitating authority in a larger structure of such authority under ultimate governmental control, and this could continue to be true after the merger or acquisition was completed. Indeed, where a merger or an acquisition is approved by the government, it would appear to be a straightforward consequence of this approval that the leaders of the new corporate entity are exercising legitimate authority in a larger structure under ultimate governmental control. Viewed in this way, mergers and acquisitions do not bring about a qualitative transformation in authority relations but rather involve, to a greater degree, the sort of changes that can take place within a single corporation when executives decide that reorganization is necessary if corporate goals are to be achieved.

Still, mergers and acquisitions can be troubling from the standpoint of legitimacy when managerial authority is understood as cooperation facilitating. The managers and employees of the acquired corporation, or those who remain, may acknowledge that acceptance of the new arrangements can be demanded of them as reasonable participants in the overall system of social cooperation that is in place in their polity, because reasonable participants in the overall system must be prepared to live with a certain amount of perceived moral error. But they could nevertheless judge the moral sacrifice involved in complying with corporate directives to be greater than was formerly the case, and regard the merger as a negative development for this reason. Facts of corporate culture are important in this connection. The moral sensibilities of the executives and employees of the acquired corporation will have been shaped in part by life in that corporation, and the new culture may grate on these sensibilities.

The issues here can be brought out most clearly by considering the case of a hostile takeover, where the senior executives, including the board of directors, of the target corporation—as well, presumably, as most employees—are opposed to its acquisition by the bidding corporation. Hostile takeovers have some of the character of conquest in the political sphere. The owners or shareholders of the target corporation may view the acquisition simply as a mutually beneficial exchange, but for the senior executives and employees, the people cooperating to maintain the acquired corporation, the process can take a form analogous to the conquest of one state by another. Directive power is seized in the face of opposition by the people who will be subject to its exercise.

Often the question of whether a hostile takeover would serve the public good will admit of reasonable disagreement. To repeat, it is necessary to distinguish reasonable moral disagreement from a mere clash of rationalizations grounded in competing personal interests. When a takeover is hostile, the members of the target corporation will usually regard their interests as threatened. But it may also be possible for members of the target corporation, reasoning competently within the perspectives provided by their distinctive life experiences, to reject the takeover on moral grounds. That is, top management, the board of directors, and the employees of the target corporation may have experiences, in their capacity as members of that corporation, that provide a basis for competently reasoned judgments that the takeover would not serve the public good.

161

Where there is reasonable moral disagreement, each side will usually be justified from its perspective in trying to bring about the result it regards as morally correct. This can involve attempting to influence the relevant governing bodies. But the parties to a reasonable disagreement can also act directly, within legal limits, to secure the result they regard as required by morality, even when this puts them in an adversarial position with respect to those who hold other reasonable views. In the case of the hostile takeover, those holding reasonable views that support the takeover could include the shareholders of the target corporation. Thus if the senior executives of the corporation reasonably judge the takeover to be contrary to the public good, they could be justified in taking actions that many shareholders find inappropriate. For example, they could make the takeover more expensive by creating a poison pill. This tactic can benefit the shareholders by raising the price that is ultimately paid for the corporation. But it can also derail negotiations, and the executives of the target corporation could create a poison pill with the specific intention of securing this result because they judge the acquisition to be contrary to the public good.

Market interactions guided by the profit motive ordinarily promote the value of social prosperity, but this is not guaranteed in the case of a hostile takeover. The takeover might affect competition in a particular industry in a way that reasonable people could regard as detrimental to social prosperity, even if the government was prepared to allow it to go forward. And values other than social prosperity, such as the advancement of knowledge or the preservation of the health of the population, could also be at issue in a proposed hostile takeover, giving competent reasoners further grounds for concluding that it would not serve the public good. Thus in the case of a hostile takeover of a media company, the executives of the target may anticipate that the bidder, if successful, will seek profit in a way that undercuts the company's role in promoting the advancement of knowledge and the development of culture.

The situation with respect to a hostile takeover, then, is as follows. It may be foreseen by all concerned that the people who possess directive power in the corporate entity that results from the takeover will be legitimately exercising a subordinate form of cooperation-facilitating authority in a larger structure under ultimate governmental control. But the senior executives and the employees of the target corporation could nevertheless be acting on competently reasoned moral judgments in attempting to prevent the takeover.[7] Normally, shareholders do not play a significant role in the management of a corporation, but they have the legal power to authorize the sale of the corporation to a bidder. So when the shareholders and the executives of the target corporation disagree about whether a proposed takeover would serve the public good, the executives may not, in the end, be able to prevail. Still, they could be acting defensibly in resisting the takeover.

The fact that it will often be possible for reasonable people to disagree about whether a hostile takeover would promote the public good deserves emphasis. This possibility has the consequence that when the decision is made by the shareholders, *they* will be exercising legislative authority. By deciding who will exercise directive power, they will be establishing a part of the conception of the public good that guides the overall cooperative effort in the polity. They must, then, consider what would actually serve the public good. They cannot simply be guided by their personal interests.

Multinational Corporations

Many corporations today operate in two or more countries. That is, although the corporation is headquartered in one country, it has operations in other countries. These multinational corporations might seem to present a problem for the theory of public capitalism that I have been presenting. On that theory, the senior executives of large, profit-seeking corporations exercise a subordinate form of cooperation-facilitating authority in a larger structure of such authority under ultimate governmental control. The basic idea is that the polity as a whole is cooperating to promote the public good, and corporate cooperation constitutes a component of the overall effort. But multinational corporations operate in a number of different polities. So under public capitalism, they must be seen as contributing to the different efforts to promote the public good underway in those polities. Further, the conceptions of the public good that guide these efforts will presumably differ from polity to polity. How, then, are we to understand the role played by the senior executives of multinational corporations?

A thorough exploration of the implications of the theory of public capitalism for international economic activity would require a separate book.[8] For present purposes, it is enough to note that under public capitalism, the senior executives of a multinational corporation exercise a subordinate form of cooperation-facilitating authority in several different countries at once. So the executives of multinational corporations will occupy a number of different subordinate roles. But as long as each government is concerned only with what happens within the country it governs, there is no reason why executives playing these different subordinate roles should confront conflicting demands. It should be noted, however, that the headquarters of a multinational corporation will constitute a subordinate center of political decision making in the home country. The government of the home country will thus be able to direct the corporation's executives to follow certain policies in other countries, when the laws of the other countries allow this, and also to insist on disengagement when the laws of another country are incompatible with the policies favored by the government of the home country.

Although a detailed examination of the international implications of the theory of public capitalism is not possible here, something can be said about how the moral considerations relevant to corporate decision making apply on a global scale. Some of the morally important social values, or their components, have a global dimension. In particular, there can be global public goods, in the technical sense described earlier, goods that cannot be provided to any part of the world without being provided to all. The amelioration of global warming would be an example. Still, it is doubtful that the notion of *the* public good applies on a global scale.

In Chapter 1, I defined the public good as consisting of an appropriate balance among the morally important social values and the requirements of private morality. What constitutes an appropriate balance will admit of reasonable disagreement. But within a given polity, a shared set of moral concepts will generally be used to mark the morally important social values and the requirements of private morality. Consequently, people who disagree about the appropriate balance among these items can be understood as disagreeing about the same thing.

This is less true on a global scale. Some of the concepts used in one country may not be used in others, with the result that the values and principles accepted differ as well. It will still be possible for the residents of one country to use its values and principles to make moral judgments on a global scale—to view the world through them—thereby generating a conception of the public good on a global scale. But the residents of some other countries may find this conception alien. It may look to people in the United States as if the global application of the individualistic values characteristic of the United States would promote the public good everywhere, but people in other countries may have a different view. Within a single country, opposing judgments of political morality do not usually have this character. Because the residents will, for the most part, be operating with the same principles and values, differing primarily about their proper interpretation and their relative weights when they conflict, opposing views will be judged mistaken but will not be found alien. It is doubtful, then, that at the current stage of the moral history of the world, the notion of the public good can be used on an international scale in the way it can on a national scale.

This point can also be made a different way. The concept of the public good may apply only within a polity, a population whose affairs are, ultimately, under the effective control of a government. Thomas Nagel's discussion of global justice is relevant here.[9] He develops an argument that the use of the concept of distributive justice is appropriate only where a government exercises coercive control over a population. Thus the moral demands that people in other countries can make on us, demands for assistance in emergencies, for example, are not properly understood as demands of justice. No government exercises coercive control over the whole population of the world. Nagel describes various institutional arrangements that have been developed to coordinate the promotion of moral values on a global scale, but he regards these arrangements as lacking the structure that would make use of the concept of distributive justice appropriate.

The view that, pending the creation of a global government, the concept of distributive justice has no global application is controversial. But it does seem problematic to speak of the *public good* with respect to a population that is not under the control of a government, and in that sense a polity.

These points bear on the management of multinational corporations in the following way. Under public capitalism, the senior executives of large, profit-seeking corporations are understood as public officials exercising a subordinate form of political authority in a larger structure of such authority that is under ultimate governmental control and oriented toward the promotion of the public good. We cannot, however, view the senior executives of multinational corporations as public officials of the world as a whole, whose task, insofar as they are given the discretion to use their own moral judgment, is to promote the public good on a global scale. It is doubtful that the concept of the public good has application on a global scale. And in any case, in the absence of a global government, there is no larger structure of cooperation-facilitating authority of the requisite kind.

The subordinate cooperation-facilitating authority exercised by the executives of multinational corporations must consequently be understood as finding its proper place within structures that are (1) under the ultimate control of particular national governments and (2) oriented toward the promotion of the public good in the countries in question. When the exercise of managerial authority contributes to more encompassing forms of political cooperation, this will be because the governments of the countries where a given corporation operates are themselves cooperating to achieve certain outcomes.

There is increasing discussion today of the possibility that the state (or the nation-state, in the sense of a member of the United

Nations) is headed for obsolescence. One of the main reasons cited is that much of what happens in a modern state is the result of international economic activity over which governments have little control. But on the theory of public capitalism that I have presented, a trend of this sort, if it is actually taking place, will have the effect of rendering illegitimate the authority exercised by the executives of multinational corporations. If it is to be legitimate, this authority must constitute a subordinate form of political authority in a larger structure that is under ultimate governmental control. Pending the emergence of a world government, this means subordination to the national governments in place in all the countries where a given corporation operates. At the present time, then, the legitimacy of the authority exercised by corporate executives presupposes the existence of a global system of robust national governments. Because the cooperation that takes place in corporations forms such a large part of political cooperation generally, it follows that in our current circumstances, a global system of robust national governments is indispensable for the proper ordering of human affairs.

NOTES

Introduction

1. I am using the concept of subordinating authority to encompass any relationship marked by the issuing of directives to people normally prepared to comply with them, regardless of what justifies, or is thought to justify, compliance. Thus the authority of an expert could take a subordinating form if its exercise involved issuing directives.

2. Christopher McMahon, *Reasonable Disagreement: A Theory of Political Morality* (Cambridge: Cambridge University Press, 2009).

3. Oliver E. Williamson, *The Economic Institutions of Capitalism: Firms, Markets, Relational Contracting* (New York: Free Press, 1985), p. 387. This approach to corporate governance was originally proposed by R. H. Coase in "The Nature of the Firm," *Economica* 4 (1937): 386–405.

4. Stephen Bainbridge, *The New Corporate Governance in Theory and Practice* (New York: Oxford University Press, 2008).

5. "Corporate governance can be characterized as the terms that firms offer investors to obtain capital on favorable terms." John R. Boatright, "Employee Governance and the Ownership of the Firm," *Business Ethics Quarterly* 14 (2004): 1–21, at p. 14.

Chapter 1

1. Ian Bremmer discusses state capitalism in *The End of the Free Market: Who Wins the War Between States and Corporations?* (New York: Portfolio, 2010).

2. For a description of what might be called a pure capitalist system, see Gerald Gaus, "The Idea and Ideal of Capitalism," in *The Oxford Handbook of Business Ethics*, ed. G. G. Brenkert and T. L. Beauchamp (New York: Oxford University Press, 2009), pp. 73–99. The public capitalism that I am proposing is not a pure capitalist system in this sense.

3. See A. M. Honoré, "Ownership," in *Oxford Essays in Jurisprudence*, ed. A. Guest (Oxford: Clarendon Press, 1961), pp. 107–47.

4. Thanks to Janine Scancarelli for this information.

5. For discussion, see William T. Allen, "Our Schizophrenic Conception of the Business Corporation," *Cardozo Law Review* 14 (1992): 261–81. The former view is known as the inherence theory because the right to incorporate is said to inhere in private property rights. The latter view is known as the concession theory because the state is understood to concede the right to incorporate, with the expectation that this will serve the state's purposes.

6. John Locke, *The Second Treatise of Government*, ed. C. B. Macpherson (Indianapolis, Ind.: Hackett, 1980), chap. V.

7. See Robert Nozick, *Anarchy, State, and Utopia* (New York: Basic Books, 1974), pp. 174–82.

8. Why isn't it enough to say, as libertarianism does, that if the parties to economic transactions respect the requirements of private morality and in that way treat each other fairly, any distribution of wealth and income that results is morally acceptable? Leaving aside the problem of providing for property within the framework of private morality—the limitations of Locke's theory were discussed earlier—economic transactions in a modern society take place against an institutional background that affects

each individual's life prospects and, in particular, what he or she will be able to obtain through market transactions. Thus the only way to determine whether people have a legitimate claim to what they can obtain from market transactions is to evaluate this institutional background itself from the standpoint of fairness.

These matters are discussed by John Rawls in "The Basic Structure as Subject" in his *Political Liberalism* (New York: Columbia University Press, 1993), pp. 275–78. Rawls says, "Under certain conditions someone's contribution to a joint venture, or to an ongoing association, can be estimated: one simply notes how the venture or association would fare without that person's joining, and the difference measures their worth to the venture or association. The attractiveness of joining to the individuals is ascertained by a comparison with their opportunities" (pp. 275–76). But, he goes on, we cannot approach in a similar way membership in a society. The society as a whole has no ends of the kind that would allow us to estimate a member's overall social worth. A political society has the end of promoting the public good, but this does not provide a basis for such an estimate. As for other opportunities, "we cannot know what we would have been like had we not belonged to [our society]" (p. 276). So to establish the fairness of the distribution of wealth and income in the society as whole we must take into account the fairness of the background institutions. What must be done to maintain a fair background appropriately constrains what people can gain from particular transactions.

Rawls's theory of "justice as fairness" provides criteria for evaluating background institutions from the standpoint of fairness, but on the view I take in this book, the question of what fairness requires with respect to the institutional background admits of reasonable disagreement.

9. Rawls calls justice the first virtue of social arrangements in *A Theory of Justice* (Cambridge Mass.: Harvard University Press, 1971), p. 3.

10. The distribution of liberty also presents issues of justice. The liberties in question are those associated with political and civil rights.

11. Graham Robb, "Cruising with Genius," *New York Review of Books* 26 February 2009, p. 34.

12. See, for example, Samuel Scheffler, *The Rejection of Consequentialism: A Philosophical Investigation of the Considerations Underlying Rival Moral Conceptions* (New York: Oxford University Press, 1984). For a more recent discussion of these issues by Scheffler, see his "Projects, Relationships, and Reasons," in *Reason and Value: Themes from the Moral Philosophy of Joseph Raz*, ed. R. J. Wallace, P. Pettit, S. Scheffler, and M. Smith (Oxford: Clarendon Press, 2004), pp. 247–69.

13. When what is at issue is the exercise of authority within a group, legitimacy presupposes the de facto ability to secure compliance. Whether one group member has reason to comply will generally depend on whether others can be expected to comply. This point receives further discussion in Chapter 3, note 4.

14. The decisions made within organizations that are not profit-seeking corporations, such as colleges and universities, can also have a substantial impact on the realization of morally important social values and thus the public good. To the extent that this is so, my argument that corporate executives should be understood as exercising a form of political authority will apply to the leaders of these other organizations as well. I say more about this in Chapter 3, but the primary focus of the argument that follows concerns the way capitalism can be public.

15. For a view of this sort, see Peter French, *Collective and Corporate Responsibility* (New York: Columbia University Press, 1984). He says, "Corporations as moral persons will have whatever privileges, rights, and duties are, in the normal course of events, accorded to all members of the moral community" (p. 32). In *Corporations and Citizenship* (Cambridge: Cambridge University Press, 2008),

NOTES TO PAGE 27

Andrew Crane, Dirk Matten, and Jeremy Moon explore the idea that corporations can be citizens. To the extent that citizens must be moral persons, the argument in the main text calls this idea into question. Crane, Matten, and Moon also discuss the converse possibility that corporations can play the role of governments with respect to the citizenry, understood as a set of human beings. This idea has some affinity with the theory of legitimate managerial authority that I develop in what follows. But Crane, Matten, and Moon are primarily interested in the possibility that corporations can perform some of the functions—for example, welfare functions—traditionally performed by governments. They note that this phenomenon is especially likely to be observed when multinational corporations operate in less-developed countries.

16. In "Responsibility Incorporated," *Ethics* 117 (2007): 171–201, Philip Pettit argues that group agents can be held morally responsible in their own right. That is, moral responsibility for what a group does is not exhausted by the responsibility of the individuals acting on behalf of the group for the actions they perform as individuals. Pettit's argument turns crucially on the claim that a group's rational pursuit of goals requires a decision procedure at the group level that is not reducible to the decision making that takes place at the individual level. In particular, the group's decisions cannot be understood as a function of the conclusions that its members, considered as individuals, reach about what the group should be doing.

The argument that I present in the main text does not concern moral responsibility. It concerns how the moral reasons for action possessed by corporations are to be understood. I argue that there can be no second level of moral reasons. The moral reasons possessed by corporations are the reasons possessed by the human beings who are their members. This conclusion is compatible with Pettit's argument. Although Pettit may be right that there must be an autonomous level of decision making if groups are to be understood as rationally pursuing their goals, what the group does as a rational agent will still depend on what the associated individuals have reason to do. This is shown in the first instance by the fact that Pettit's argument is aimed at the individuals who comprise his group agents. They must act on the reasons he identifies for adopting the decision procedure he recommends. In addition, the reasons tracked by the group decision making that Pettit describes will be "human" reasons, reasons that bear on how the associated individuals should organize their affairs. The two decision procedures that Pettit distinguishes constitute two different ways of extracting conclusions from such reasons. I discuss these points in more detail in "Pettit on Collectivizing Reason," *Social Theory and Practice* 32 (2006): 431–49.

Chapter 2

1. In *The Corrosion of Character: The Personal Consequences of Work in the New Capitalism* (New York: Norton, 1998), chap. 6, Richard Sennett characterizes the team structure found in some modern corporations as one marked by "power without authority." But he seems to be referring only to the role of lower-level managers who function as team leaders and who are regarded in this model as having a status like that of the captain of a sports team. The focus of the present book is the role played in a modern capitalist society by the senior executives of large corporations, and I believe that in all such corporations, the senior executives can be regarded as exercising what I have called "subordinating authority," marked by deference to directives. In *The Culture of the New Capitalism* (New Haven, Conn.: Yale University Press, 2006), Sennett seems to agree, saying, "[I]n a flexible organization, power becomes concentrated at the center; the institution's central processing unit sets the tasks, judges results, expands and shrinks the firm" (p. 51).

2. See, for example, Armen A. Alchian and Harold Demsetz,

"Production, Information Costs, and Economic Organization," *American Economic Review* 62 (1972): 777–95. Alchian and Demsetz explain the capitalist firm as a response to the difficulty of metering inputs in the context of team production. Thanks to Jeff Moriarty for raising the issues discussed in this and the preceding paragraph.

3. For discussion of the deference associated with authority, see Joseph Raz, "Authority and Justification," *Philosophy and Public Affairs* 14 (1985): 3–29, and my *Authority and Democracy: A General Theory of Government and Management* (Princeton, N.J.: Princeton University Press, 1994), pp. 27–33.

4. American Law Institute, *Restatement (Third) of Agency*, 2006, 7.07 (3) (a).

5. Ibid., 1.01.

6. Ibid., 1.04 (5).

7. Ibid., 8.09 (2).

8. See T. M. Scanlon, *What We Owe to Each Other* (Cambridge, Mass.: Harvard University Press, 1998), chap. 7.

9. This way of construing the moral obligations associated with employment, according to which they are owed to the other members of the corporation rather than to the corporation understood as a separate moral person, has some affinity with the "nexus of contracts" model of the corporation used by many management theorists, including Stephen Bainbridge. (See the discussion in the Introduction.) Bainbridge emphasizes the importance of implicit contracts, and these can be understood in terms of the induction of reliance. The nexus he has in mind, however, includes shareholders and other stakeholders, as well as the employees and top management, all of whom contract with the board of directors, viewed as a group of cooperating individuals rather than as a distinct social entity. By contrast, I distinguish the members of a corporation from others who have an interest in what it does. The members are the people who are parties to the relations of sub-

ordinating authority found within the corporation. On the view I am proposing, then, the senior executives of a corporation—in which group I include, as I have said, the board of directors—are members of it.

10. I first argued for the normative duality of management in *Authority and Democracy*, pp. 15–18.

11. One right of ownership is the right to manage the use of an item by others. But this is not a right to direct others in a sense that entails an obligation on the part of those directed to comply. It is a right to wield the directive power created by control of a piece of productive property, and its normative force lies in the exclusion from this activity of other people who might also want to wield that power.

12. In a discussion of these ideas at the University of Calgary, it was suggested that there may be cases in which property rights enable an owner to direct positive actions. The examples proposed involved the rental of apartments or cars. I am inclined, however, to think that in such cases the moral reason to perform any positive actions directed by the owners is provided by the rental agreement rather than by property rights. It is also worth noting that in the examples I have given, riding in someone's car or visiting his house, something like gratitude for hospitality might give one a moral reason to comply with a directive from the owner. But again, the moral work will not be done by property rights.

13. As mentioned in Chapter 1, note 8, the status of distributive justice as a morally important social value is connected with the fact that background institutions have a profound effect in each individual's life prospects and thus on what he or she can obtain through market transactions. In general, only governments are in a position to modify background institutions to promote distributive justice, so its promotion is in the first instance the responsibility of governments. But issues of distributive justice are ultimately issues of social fairness, and such issues can arise within smaller

cooperative undertakings in a way that is relevant to the fairness of the distribution of wealth and income in the larger society.

14. One reason for this is that the extensive use of antibiotics fosters the evolution of drug-resistant pathogens. The treatment received by animals meant for food might also be regarded as morally objectionable independently of any effects on human welfare. In this book, I am focusing on the consequences of corporate practices for a set of moral considerations grounded, ultimately, in human well-being: the principles of private morality and the morally important social values. But moral considerations related to the treatment of animals, or of the planet as a whole, may also be regarded by some employees as generating reasons for action that can outweigh a promissory obligation to their employers.

15. For discussion of the concept of integrity, see Bernard Williams, "A Critique of Utilitarianism," in *Utilitarianism For and Against*, by J. J. C. Smart and Bernard Williams (Cambridge: Cambridge University Press, 1973), pp. 108–18, and "Utilitarianism and Moral Self-indulgence," in *Moral Luck*, ed. B. Williams (Cambridge: Cambridge University Press, 1981), pp. 40–53. Williams discusses cases in which considerations of integrity might be thought to justify an agent in declining to perform a morally repugnant action that would prevent a worse situation. The most famous of these involves being confronted with a situation in which twenty innocent people are threatened with execution, and you could save the lives of nineteen of them by shooting one of them yourself. Williams argues that it is not obvious that morality would require killing the one and identifies the countervailing consideration as the fact that doing so would compromise your integrity as a moral agent. But the idea that one can have a strong moral reason to decline to become involved in activities one regards as morally objectionable has broader application, as the example of purchasing clothing made in a sweatshop shows.

Reasons of integrity display a certain amount of interpersonal variability. An action that one person would judge to compromise her integrity may not be understood in this way by another person. In cases of the kind we are considering, one important reason for this variability is that competent reasoners can come to different conclusions about the moral character of the outcomes produced by a collective endeavor. This reasonable disagreement is discussed further below.

16. The idea that considerations of integrity can justify an employee's declining to comply with a managerial directive resembles in certain respects Michael Davis's complicity theory of whistle-blowing. See his "Some Paradoxes of Whistleblowing," *Business and Professional Ethics Journal* 15 (1996): 3–18, and "Whistleblowing," in *The Oxford Handbook of Practical Ethics*, ed. Hugh LaFollette (New York: Oxford University Press, 2005), pp. 539–63. On the complicity theory, the whistle-blower blows the whistle to avoid complicity in what she justifiably and correctly takes to be wrongdoing. There are some differences between the two views, however. First, Davis's whistle-blowers reveal wrongdoing that derives from the work they do in the organization, and this seems to be understood relatively narrowly. By contrast, I have suggested that simply by doing their jobs, all employees are engaged in any wrongdoing that can be ascribed to the corporation. Second, the employees I am envisaging don't typically blow the whistle. What they find objectionable may be public knowledge. Rather they continue to do their jobs in the normal way, despite any moral reservations they may have about corporate policies, because the sacrifice involved in acting on their moral convictions would be too great. This social phenomenon is discussed in more detail in the next section.

17. I explain how reasonable disagreement can fail to be perceived as such by the parties in *Reasonable Disagreement: A Theory of Political Morality* (Cambridge: Cambridge University Press, 2009), esp. chaps. 1–3.

18. The qualification concerning competent reasoning is important. The fact that only coercive sanctions move the morally irresponsible residents of a state—for example, potential criminals—does not threaten the legitimacy of the government even if this group constitutes a significant subset of the population. As the case of philosophically sophisticated anarchism shows, however, legitimacy is in a way a happy accident. It is conceivable that all the members of a polity could, through competent reasoning, become sophisticated anarchists. But as things are, the tenability of anarchism admits of reasonable disagreement, and most people whose cooperative capacities are functioning properly do not come to anarchistic conclusions.

19. The application of directive power to the group as a whole will usually be necessary to provide each member with assurance that the others will comply. I will discuss this point further in the next chapter.

20. It is relevant to this argument that the employees of a corporation are normally hired to perform particular jobs, which themselves take the form of a coordinated structure within the corporation. The role of explicit direction is to give further refinement to the coordination implicit in the structure. So if a significant number of employees can competently judge that they lack sufficient reason to comply with managerial directives—which is to say, to do their jobs—the failures of coordination that call legitimacy into question will be especially likely.

21. It should be noted that the argument presented in this section concerns moral wrongness, not responsibility. The argument has turned on the possibility that a competently reasoning employee could conclude that complying with managerial directives was something she had sufficient moral reason not to do—which is to say, the possibility that the employee could judge complying to be morally wrong. The issue of wrongdoing must be distinguished from issues of responsibility and blame. In "Respon-

sibility Incorporated," *Ethics* 117 (2007): 171–201, Philip Pettit distinguishes members of a corporation from what he calls "enactors," who can be held responsible as individuals for particular morally problematic actions of the corporation. Enactors are usually members, but many members will not be enactors. Many employees who would, if reasoning competently on the basis of full information, judge themselves to be acting wrongly in complying with managerial directives might not have the status of enactors. They might, for example, be unable to do anything to prevent the corporate actions they found impermissible. But although such employees could not be held responsible for the corporate actions they found morally objectionable, they might still, when reasoning competently, judge themselves to be acting wrongly when complying with managerial directives.

22. In the corporate case, the "promise" to pay the employee can be understood as an undertaking by the corporation as a legal person, which gives rise to a legal obligation. This is then discharged by certain members of the corporation who judge that they have sufficient reason to maintain the legal structures constitutive of the corporation.

23. The argument I have given concerns the standard arrangement in which pay is provided after a certain amount of work has been performed. If pay is provided in advance, employment will still involve a promise to comply with directives in return for pay, and the promise can still be outweighed. Again, though, we must ask what happens next. As before, the employee may be justified in continuing to comply because the sacrifice involved in declining to comply—in this case, not forgoing future pay but returning part of the pay already received—is more than consequentialist considerations can require. And as before, this just gives the employer directive power, not legitimate authority.

In "The Public Authority of the Managers of Private Corporations," in *The Oxford Handbook of Business Ethics*, ed. G. G. Brenkert and T. L. Beauchamp (New York: Oxford University Press, 2009), I say that the argument that a promissory obligation cannot ground managerial authority does not require the step presented in this section, but I now think it does.

24. As Upton Sinclair put it in a well-known quote, "It is difficult to get a man to understand something when his salary depends on his not understanding it." (*I, Candidate for Governor: And How I Got Licked* [Berkeley: University of California Press, 1994], p. 109.) **181**

25. George A. Akerlof and Robert J. Shiller, *Animal Spirits: How Human Psychology Drives the Economy, and Why It Matters for Global Capitalism* (Princeton, N.J.: Princeton University Press, 2009), p. 106.

Chapter 3

1. A. John Simmons, *Moral Principles and Political Obligations* (Princeton, N.J.: Princeton University Press, 1979).

2. The results that experimental game theorists have obtained in the so-called ultimatum game, and in similar games, can be interpreted as showing that humans are disposed to make concessions in cooperative contexts, even when there is no threat of punishment for not doing so, and to punish the failure to make concessions even at significant personal cost. For discussion of the ultimatum game, see Richard H. Thaler, "The Ultimatum Game," *Journal of Economic Perspectives* 2 (Autumn 1988): 195–206. A general survey of relevant experimental results can be found in Samuel Bowles and Herbert Gintis, *A Cooperative Species: Human Reciprocity and Its Evolution* (Princeton, N.J.: Princeton University Press, 2011), chap. 3. Bowles and Gintis take these results to show that humans are not purely self-interested but rather have social preferences of various kinds.

3. I discuss fairness in "Disagreement about Fairness" in *Philosophical Topics* (forthcoming).

4. The idea that the justification for compliance must be inde-pendent of coercive sanctions requires clarification. Reasonable people will comply with directives intended to provide a basis for cooperation only if they have good reason to believe that enough others will comply to secure the cooperative benefit. Common knowledge, in the relevant group, that the source of the directives possesses directive power can provide this assurance, and the use of coercive sanctions is one form this directive power can take. But where coercive sanctions are used, the members of the group may still have sufficient *coercion-independent* reason to comply. The sanctions, by giving each member good reason to believe the *others* will comply, can make it possible for him to comply on the ground of the reasonableness of doing so.

5. In extreme cases, people who regard a particular law, or set of laws, as contrary to the public good may resort to civil disobe-dience. But because people engaged in civil disobedience accept the legal consequences of disobedience, there is a sense in which they are not demanding a concession from the other cooperators.

6. It is relevant to the reasonableness of the procedures of liber-al democracy that the decisions that are made are not permanent. Thus those who regard them as mistaken can work to overturn them in the future.

7. As we saw in Chapter 2, the function of subordinating author-ity, exercised over the members of a collective agent, is to secure coordinated action by the members. This requires that almost all of them be able to judge, when reasoning competently, that they have sufficient coercion-independent reason to comply with the directives they are receiving. I have argued that this condition can be met in the political case if almost all the members of the polity in question regard the operative decision-making procedure—the form of government—as providing a reasonable way of resolving reasonable disagreement. When this is not the case, the govern-ment will not be fully legitimate in the sense we have been explor-

ing. But it is useful to distinguish two forms a situation of this sort can take. The form of government may be competently rejected by a substantial minority of the population, yet still be accepted by the majority, or it may be competently rejected by a majority.

In the first situation, the government can claim justification of a kind for maintaining political control. The justification is that if **183** the form of government preferred by the minority were instituted, without a corresponding change of mind in the majority, the situation would be even worse from the standpoint of justified compliance. In *Reasonable Disagreement: A Theory of Political Morality* (Cambridge: Cambridge University Press, 2009), chap. 5, fourth section, I suggest that when a form of government that is accepted only by a minority of the members of a polity is imposed on the rest of the population, we have *despotism*. It should be noted, however, that even when the existing form of government can be defended on the ground that instituting the alternative preferred by the minority would bring about despotism, it is still incumbent upon all reasonable members of the polity to try to devise a set of decision procedures that is acceptable to almost everyone—that is, to create a government that can meet the standard for full legitimacy.

8. In Chapter 2, it was suggested that the reasonable views on a given question of political morality can be understood as those that would survive shared deliberation conducted in good faith. Because shared deliberation is always a possibility, the unreasonableness of much actual political opinion is, in principle, a correctable problem.

9. If, as we are supposing, questions of political morality admit of reasonable disagreement, there will be several different competently reasoned ways of understanding such a balance. The assumption being made here is that one of them will be guiding political cooperation. In general, a particular political decision will determine the organization of a specific aspect of the overall

cooperative endeavor, so the disagreements that are resolved will concern how that aspect should be organized.

10. Grounding the legitimacy of managerial authority in the concept of reasonableness does not preclude the possibility of a promissory obligation to comply with managerial directives of the sort discussed in Chapter 2. But considerations of reasonableness can justify compliance when a promissory obligation is unable to do this. And the argument in Chapter 2 makes it likely that where dissent is so radical that considerations of reasonableness are not able to secure compliance, a promissory obligation would not be able to secure it either. So such obligations can be disregarded.

11. The hierarchical framework is maintained by the cooperation of all the members of the society, so there is a sense in which the placing of people in different positions is a collective act. But it does not involve a choice among alternative arrangements. Rather it involves the reproduction of what history has bequeathed.

John Locke gives expression to the concept of autonomy in the political sense, without using that word, when he says, "To understand political power right and derive it from its original, we must consider what state all men are naturally in, and that is a state of perfect freedom to order their actions and dispose of their possessions and persons as they think fit, within the bounds of the law of nature, without asking leave or depending upon the will of any other man." *The Second Treatise of Government*, ed. C. B. Macpherson (Indianapolis, Ind.: Hackett, 1980), sec. 4.

12. In "Employee Governance and the Ownership of the Firm," *Business Ethics Quarterly* 14 (2004): 1–21, John R. Boatright argues that the debate about corporate democracy has been distorted by the idea that it requires giving employees ownership rights of the same kind as shareholders—that it requires shareholders to share their ownership rights with employees. He proposes that even under current arrangements of corporate governance, employees

can be understood as having ownership rights of a kind. Further, these rights bring with them a claim to participate in ownership-appropriate ways, which primarily concern the organization of the workplace, in corporate governance. The result is that a place is found for employee governance while leaving shareholders in exclusive possession of the rights they have under current governance arrangements. However, the quote that appears in note 5 to the Introduction suggests that Boatright's thinking about corporate governance is guided ultimately by considerations of economic efficiency. Under public capitalism, economic efficiency and the associated value of social prosperity must be balanced against further components of the public good. This may support forms of employee participation that do not conform to Boatright's picture.

13. See Henry S. Richardson, *Democratic Autonomy: Public Reasoning about the Ends of Policy* (New York: Oxford University Press, 2002). Richardson gives the example of the Biaggi Amendment to the Urban Mass Transit Act of 1970. This mandated that steps be taken to make mass transit systems accessible to the elderly and the disabled, but it was left to the Department of Transportation to sort through different definitions of access and craft a specific policy.

14. See, for example, Richardson, *Democratic Autonomy,* chap. 16, and Philip Pettit, *A Theory of Freedom* (New York: Oxford University Press, 2001), chap. 7, esp. pp. 169–71.

15. For an overview of the stakeholder idea, see Thomas Donaldson and Lee E. Preston, "The Stakeholder Theory of the Corporation: Concepts, Evidence, and Implications," *Academy of Management Review* 20 (1995): 65–91.

16. In *Entrepreneurs and Democracy: A Political Theory of Corporate Governance* (Cambridge: Cambridge University Press, 2008), Pierre-Yves Gomez and Harry Korine characterize the democratic nature of modern society as one of increasing fragmentation. For

the modern business corporation, this takes the form in the first instance of fragmentation in the concerns of the shareholders. These authors also posit a countervailing principle of social organization, the entrepreneurial principle. According to this view successful corporate governance requires the entrepreneurial harnessing of shareholder fragmentation in the pursuit of economic performance. Gomez and Korine acknowledge the force of public opinion, but they appear to think that it will be satisfied if economic performance—what I have called the promotion of social prosperity—is achieved in the face of this increasing fragmentation.

Under public capitalism, by contrast, social prosperity is just one component of the public good, and the ultimate criterion of successful corporate governance is promotion of the public good as a whole. It follows that corporate decision making must be responsive in some way to morally important social values other than social prosperity—or, to be more precise, to reasonable views about what the public good as a whole requires.

17. I thank an anonymous referee for pointing out the need for clarification here.

18. We should be clear about what is involved in the resolution of reasonable moral disagreement. It is not necessarily a matter of striking a balance among all the reasonable views. Where a particular issue admits of reasonable disagreement, there will be a zone of reasonable disagreement consisting of all the reasonable positions that can be taken on that issue. Resolving reasonable moral disagreement is a matter of selecting for implementation one of the positions falling within the zone. This can involve finding a middle point, but it need not. The method of majority rule is plausibly regarded as a reasonable way of resolving reasonable disagreement, and if in a particular case a majority holds a view that falls on one side of the issue, that view will be selected for implementation.

Chapter 4

1. Adam Smith, *An Inquiry into the Nature and Causes of the Wealth of Nations*, ed. E. Cannon (New York: Modern Library, 1994), bk. IV, chap. 2.

2. A distribution is Pareto optimal when it is not possible to make anyone better off without making someone else worse off. Pareto optimality is a measure of efficiency. If it is possible to make someone better off without making someone else worse off, resources are not being efficiently used.

Because the idea that there can be a connection between the pursuit of profit and benefits to the larger society does not require the legal concept of a corporation, I will sometimes speak of "firms" in what follows.

3. Thomas Hobbes, *Leviathan*, ed. E. Curley (Indianapolis, Ind.: Hackett, 1994), p. 76.

4. Joseph Heath, "An Adversarial Ethic for Business: Or When Sun-Tzu Met the Stakeholder," *Journal of Business Ethics* 72 (2007): 359–74.

5. Joseph Schumpeter, *Capitalism, Socialism, and Democracy* (New York: Harper, 2008).

6. The special circumstances are primarily those in which the infliction of harm is required for self-defense or for the defense of others.

7. I use the term layoff to refer to any termination of employment that is not for cause, so there is no implication that the affected employees will eventually be rehired by the company involved.

8. For a discussion of the doctrine of employment at will, see John J. McCall and Patricia H. Werhane, "Employment at Will and Employee Rights," in *The Oxford Handbook of Business Ethics*, ed. G. G. Brenkert and T. L. Beauchamp (New York: Oxford University Press, 2009), pp. 602–27. McCall and Werhane present reasons for

supposing that the termination of employment can have indirect costs that affect how financially beneficial it will actually be for firms.

9. Corporations may retain employees when this is financially disadvantageous in the short term because executives judge it to

be advantageous in the long term. They might expect business to pick up in the future and think that training new people would be more costly than keeping the employees they have. But this reason for forgoing layoffs is independent of the requirement of mutual aid. It is also worth mentioning that a situation could arise in which an employee's leaving a particular employer would have devastating consequences for the employer. But this case is like divorce. The employee is permitted to leave if remaining in employment would force him or her to incur substantial personal costs.

10. Fundamentally, autonomy is self-governance. In the philosophical literature, this is often understood as an individual's being able to endorse, or identify with, the sources of motivation that actually shape her life. A nonautonomous individual is thus someone who is, in a certain way, alienated from herself. This kind of autonomy is not relevant to our concerns here. Someone who is unable to identify with what moves her can still be allowed by others, or the larger society, to direct her own life.

11. There can be cases in which someone would be reluctant to participate in a plan because of a feature that benefits him. He might find being benefited in that way demeaning, for example. In such cases, respect for autonomy requires revealing the feature. For simplicity, I will leave this complication aside.

What is planned is what is intended, and what is intended is often contrasted with what is merely foreseen. The foreseen consequences of carrying out a plan may also provide reasons for or against participating in that plan. But this complication, too, can be set aside. If a planner intends a potential participant to remain ignorant of a foreseen consequence of carrying out the plan, this will be a part of the plan and thus must be divulged if autonomy is to be respected. So in effect, respect for autonomy precludes such intentions.

12. Intuition does not seem to support the idea that respect for the buyer's autonomy requires that she be informed of the use that the seller will make of the money he receives. This may be because money is fungible. Thus it makes no sense to ascribe a specific use to the particular dollars received in a sale.

13. The law of agency contains a provision of this kind concerning the protection of interests. According to the *Restatement*, "A principal has a duty to deal with the agent fairly and in good faith, including a duty to provide the agent with information about risks of physical harm or pecuniary loss that the principal knows, or has reason to know, or should know are present in the agent's work but unknown to the agent." American Law Institute, *Restatement (Third) of Agency* 2006, 8.15.

14. Thomas Nagel, "Ruthlessness in Public Life," in his Mortal Questions (Cambridge: Cambridge University Press, 1979), pp. 75–90. The essay can also be found in S. Hampshire, ed., *Public and Private Morality* (Cambridge: Cambridge University Press, 1979). The other essays in this collection are relevant as well.

15. See Nagel, "Ruthlessness in Public Life," p. 84. The impartiality required by public morality prohibits governmental officials from using their positions to advance their own interests, but more generally it requires them to act from a defensible conception of the public good. So using their positions to do favors for *other* people—for example, political supporters or campaign contributors—is equally unacceptable from the standpoint of impartiality.

16. These points have implications for staffing. The owner-managers of a small business, who have a prerogative in private morality to take actions that are suboptimal from the standpoint

of morally important social values, are free to hire friends and relatives even if they are not the best people for the job. But corporate executives, as public officials, must act from a defensible conception of the public good, and nepotism and cronyism are contrary to the impartiality required by the implicit morality of the market.

Chapter 5

1. John Stuart Mill, *Utilitarianism, in Classics of Moral and Political Theory*, 4th ed., ed. M. Morgan (Indianapolis, Ind.: Hackett, 2005), pp. 995–1028, at 999. The components of well-being that I have listed are taken from James Griffin, *Well-Being: Its Meaning, Measurement, and Moral Importance* (New York: Oxford University Press, 1989), pp. 67–68. Griffin presents them as components of an ideal of human flourishing. Another component mentioned by Griffin is enjoyment. A life that lacks enjoyment cannot be a flourishing life. Fully realizing one of the components of human well-being may require accepting the reduced realization of another. But a life completely lacking in any of these components of well-being will normally be deficient from the standpoint of human flourishing. If we understand enjoyment as pleasure in the satisfaction of wants, the significance of Griffin's full list of components of human well-being is that a good life will contain more than pleasure in the satisfaction of wants, and accommodating these other elements may involve accepting a lower overall level of such satisfaction.

2. Of course, this problem is not confined to capitalist systems. In any system, the people who benefit from the operation of a particular productive enterprise or the pursuit of a particular economic policy will resist arguments that the public good would be served by changes that reduce those benefits. So securing genuine shared deliberation in the economic arena will be a challenge whether a society has a capitalist system or not.

The discussion in the text concerns the form that the arguments made by corporate executives should take. The role of financial contributions to politicians in securing a hearing for these arguments, and in influencing their acceptance, was discussed in Chapter 3, in the section "The Nature of Corporate Subordination." As was noted there, this practice can reverse the relations of subordination that characterize public capitalism, thus depriving corporate executives of legitimate authority.

3. John Rawls, *Political Liberalism* (New York: Columbia University Press, 1993), p. 57.

4. I don't mean to single out cookies. To say that items of a particular kind have no independent moral value is to say that, although their production and consumption contributes to the value of social prosperity, it makes no direct contribution to any of the other components of the public good. Products and services that have no independent moral value are produced simply because people want them enough to pay the cost of producing them.

5. In "Value Maximization, Stakeholder Theory, and the Corporate Objective Function," *Business Ethics Quarterly* 12 (2002): 235–56, Michael C. Jenson argues that managerial decisions should be evaluated solely on the basis of their effect on the long-run market value of the firm. The alternative he discusses involves evaluating managerial decisions on the basis of their success in accommodating the concerns of all the firm's stakeholders. Jensen argues that successful management requires a single-valued criterion of success, and that stakeholder theory, which calls upon managers to balance the interests of different stakeholder groups, cannot provide this. In their interesting paper "Stakeholder Theory, Corporate Governance and Public Management: What Can the History of State-Run Enterprises Teach Us in the Post-Enron Era?" *Journal of Business Ethics* 53 (2004): 247–65, Joseph Heath and Wayne Norman argue in a similar vein that stakeholder theory, by giving managers the status of agents

191

responsible to multiple principals, generates intractable agency problems.

As was described in Chapter 3, under public capitalism the performance of corporate executives is appropriately evaluated on the basis of the contributions they make, in a subordinate capacity, to the promotion of the public good. The articles just cited can be understood as arguing that maximizing firm value is the most effective way for corporate executives to promote the public good. The idea, presumably, would be that maximizing firm value promotes social prosperity, which is a component of the public good. But for public capitalism, issues concerning the public good admit of reasonable disagreement. And some reasonable members of capitalist polities may conclude that the maximization of firm value does not in fact promote social prosperity or that corporate decision making should be sensitive to other moral considerations as well.

6. The conceptual-cum-social process is discussed in my *Reasonable Disagreement: A Theory of Political Morality* (Cambridge: Cambridge University Press, 2009), chap. 4, third section.

7. A hostile takeover bid is a particular kind of unsolicited takeover bid, one that is not welcomed by the management of the target corporation. Unsolicited takeover bids are discussed by Stephen Bainbridge in *The New Corporate Governance in Theory and Practice* (New York: Oxford University Press, 2008), pp. 134–53. He defends the existence of legal mechanisms that allow hostile bids to be resisted, but his sole criterion is economic efficiency.

8. In *Corporations and Citizenship* (Cambridge: Cambridge University Press, 2008), Andrew Crane, Dirk Matten, and Jeremy Moon provide a helpful overview of the complex role that multinational corporations play in the countries where they operate. See, especially, chaps. 3 and 7.

9. Thomas Nagel, "The Problem of Global Justice," *Philosophy and Public Affairs* 33 (2005): 113–47.

WORKS CITED

Akerlof, George A. and Robert J. Shiller. *Animal Spirits: How Human Psychology Drives the Economy, and Why It Matters for Global Capitalism.* Princeton, N.J.: Princeton University Press, 2009.

Alchian, Armen A. and Harold Demsetz. "Production, Information Costs, and Economic Organization." *American Economic Review* 62 (1972): 777–95.

Allen, William T. "Our Schizophrenic Conception of the Business Corporation." *Cardozo Law Review* 14 (1992): 261–81.

American Law Institute. *Restatement (Third) of Agency.* 2006.

Bainbridge, Stephen. *The New Corporate Governance in Theory and Practice.* New York: Oxford University Press, 2008.

Boatright, John R. "Employee Governance and the Ownership of the Firm." *Business Ethics Quarterly* 14 (2004): 1–21.

Bowles, Samuel and Herbert Gintis. *A Cooperative Species: Human Reciprocity and Its Evolution.* Princeton, N.J.: Princeton University Press, 2011.

Bremmer, Ian. *The End of the Free Market: Who Wins the War Between States and Corporations?* New York: Portfolio, 2010.

Brenkert, George G. and Tom L. Beauchamp. *The Oxford Handbook of Business Ethics* New York: Oxford University Press, 2009.

Coase, R. H. "The Nature of the Firm." *Economica* 4 (1937): 386–405.

Crane, Andrew, Dirk Matten, and Jeremy Moon. *Corporations and Citizenship.* Cambridge: Cambridge University Press, 2008.

Davis, Michael. "Some Paradoxes of Whistleblowing." *Business and Professional Ethics Journal* 15 (1996): 3–18.

———. "Whistleblowing." In *The Oxford Handbook of Practical Ethics*, ed. Hugh LaFollette. New York: Oxford University Press, 2005, pp. 539–63.

Donaldson, Thomas and Lee E. Preston. "The Stakeholder Theory of the Corporation: Concepts, Evidence, and Implications." *Academy of Management Review* 20 (1995): 65–91.

French, Peter. *Collective and Corporate Responsibility.* New York: Columbia University Press, 1984.

Gaus, Gerald. "The Idea and Ideal of Capitalism." In *The Oxford Handbook of Business Ethics*, ed. G. G. Brenkert and T. L. Beauchamp, pp. 73–99.

Gomez, Pierre-Yves and Harry Korine. *Entrepreneurs and Democracy: A Political Theory of Corporate Governance.* Cambridge: Cambridge University Press, 2008.

Griffin, James. *Well-Being: Its Meaning, Measurement, and Moral Importance.* New York: Oxford University Press, 1989.

Hampshire, Stuart, ed. *Public and Private Morality.* Cambridge: Cambridge University Press, 1979.

Heath, Joseph. "An Adversarial Ethic for Business: Or When Sun-Tzu Met the Stakeholder." *Journal of Business Ethics* 72 (2007): 359–74.

Heath, Joseph and Wayne Norman. "Stakeholder Theory, Corporate Governance and Public Management: What Can the History of State-Run Enterprises Teach Us in the Post-Enron Era?" *Journal of Business Ethics* 53 (2004): 247–65.

Hobbes, Thomas. *Leviathan.* Ed. E. Curley. Indianapolis, Ind.: Hackett, 1994.

Honoré, A. M. "Ownership." In *Oxford Essays in Jurisprudence*, ed. A. Guest. Oxford: Clarendon Press, 1961, pp. 107–47.

Jensen, Michael C. "Value Maximization, Stakeholder Theory, and the Corporate Objective Function." *Business Ethics Quarterly* 12 (2002): 235–56.

Locke, John. *The Second Treatise of Government*. Ed. C. B. Macpherson. Indianapolis, Ind.: Hackett, 1980.

McCall, John J. and Patricia A. Werhane. "Employment at Will and Employee Rights." In *The Oxford Handbook of Business Ethics*, ed. G. G. Brenkert and T. L. Beauchamp, pp. 602–27.

McMahon, Christopher. "Morality and the Invisible Hand." *Philosophy and Public Affairs* 10 (1981): 247–77.

———. *Authority and Democracy: A General Theory of Government and Management*. Princeton, N.J.: Princeton University Press, 1994.

———. "Pettit on Collectivizing Reason." *Social Theory and Practice* 32 (2006): 431–49.

———. "The Public Authority of the Managers of Private Corporations." In *The Oxford Handbook of Business Ethics*, ed. G. G. Brenkert and T. L. Beauchamp, pp. 100–125.

———. *Reasonable Disagreement: A Theory of Political Morality*. Cambridge: Cambridge University Press, 2009.

———. "Disagreement about Fairness." In *Philosophical Topics* (forthcoming).

Mill, John Stuart. *Utilitarianism*. In *Classics of Moral and Political Theory*, ed. M. Morgan. 4th ed. Indianapolis, Ind.: Hackett, 2005, pp. 995–1028.

Nagel, Thomas. *Mortal Questions*. Cambridge: Cambridge University Press, 1979.

———. "The Problem of Global Justice." *Philosophy and Public Affairs* 33 (2005): 113–47.

Nozick, Robert. *Anarchy, State, and Utopia*. New York: Basic Books, 1974.

Pettit, Philip. *A Theory of Freedom.* Oxford: Oxford University Press, 2001.

——. "Responsibility Incorporated." *Ethics* 117 (2007): 171–201.

Rawls, John. *A Theory of Justice.* Cambridge, Mass.: Harvard University Press, 1971.

——. *Political Liberalism.* New York: Columbia University Press, 1993.

Raz, Joseph. "Authority and Justification." *Philosophy and Public Affairs* 14 (1985): 3–29.

Richardson, Henry S. *Democratic Autonomy: Public Reasoning about the Ends of Policy.* New York: Oxford University Press, 2002.

Robb, Graham. "Cruising with Genius." *New York Review of Books* 26 February 2009.

Scanlon, T. M. *What We Owe to Each Other.* Cambridge, Mass.: Harvard University Press, 1998.

Scheffler, Samuel. *The Rejection of Consequentialism: A Philosophical Investigation of the Considerations Underlying Rival Moral Conceptions.* New York: Oxford University Press, 1984.

——. "Projects, Relationships, and Reasons." In *Reason and Value: Themes from the Moral Philosophy of Joseph Raz*, ed. R. J. Wallace, P. Pettit, S. Scheffler, and M. Smith. Oxford: Clarendon Press, 2004, pp. 247–69.

Schumpeter, Joseph. *Capitalism, Socialism, and Democracy.* New York: Harper, 2008.

Sennett, Richard. *The Corrosion of Character: The Personal Consequences of Work in the New Capitalism.* New York: Norton, 1998.

——. *The Culture of the New Capitalism.* New Haven, Conn.: Yale University Press, 2006.

Simmons, A. John. *Moral Principles and Political Obligations.* Princeton, N.J.: Princeton University Press, 1979.

Sinclair, Upton. *I, Candidate for Governor: And How I Got Licked.* Berkeley: University of California Press, 1994.

Smith, Adam. *An Inquiry into the Nature and Causes of the Wealth of Nations.* Ed. E. Cannon. New York.: Modern Library, 1994.

Thaler, Richard H. "The Ultimatum Game." *Journal of Economic Perspectives* 2 (Autumn 1988): 195–206.

Williams, Bernard. "A Critique of Utilitarianism." In *Utilitarianism for and Against*, ed. J. J. C. Smart and Bernard Williams. Cambridge: Cambridge University Press, 1973, pp. 108–18.

———. "Utilitarianism and Moral Self-indulgence." In *Moral Luck*, ed. B. Williams. Cambridge: Cambridge University Press, 1981, pp. 40–53.

Williamson, Oliver E. *The Economic Institutions of Capitalism: Firms, Markets, Relational Contracting.* New York: Free Press, 1985.

INDEX

ACKNOWLEDGMENTS

THIS BOOK REPRESENTS the latest stage of a philosophical project that I have been pursuing intermittently for many years. I first explored the idea that corporate executives function as public officials in "Morality and the Invisible Hand," which appeared in *Philosophy and Public Affairs* 10, no. 3 (Summer 1981): 247–77. Chapter 4 is based on that article. I first argued that corporate executives should be understood as exercising a kind of political authority in *Authority and Democracy: A General Theory of Government and Management*, published by Princeton University Press in 1994. I returned to that topic in 2009 with "The Public Authority of the Managers of Private Corporations," which is included in *The Oxford Handbook of Business Ethics*, edited by George Brenkert and Tom Beauchamp. Chapters 2 and 3 reformulate and expand the argument of that paper.

My most recent reengagement with these issues began with an invitation from Jeffery Smith to participate in a symposium on my book *Authority and Democracy* at a meeting of the Society for Business Ethics in San Francisco in 2005. I would like to thank him and the other participants, Nien-hê Hsieh, Jeffrey Moriarty, and J. (Hans) van Oosterhout, for their comments. The symposium was published in the *Journal of Business Ethics* 71 (April 2007). I would also like to thank the editors of the *Oxford*

Handbook for their invitation to contribute to that volume and for their assistance with my contribution.

Jeff Moriarty and two anonymous readers for the University of Pennsylvania Press provided instructive comments on earlier drafts of the present book. These comments included bringing to my attention some of the books and articles on business ethics, which is not my primary area of specialization, cited in this book. Where what I say here conflicts with any of my earlier work, it should be understood as correcting that work.

Finally, I have received helpful assistance at different stages in the process of completing this book from Erin Graham, the Business and Economics Editor at Penn Press, and I have benefited from the copyediting of Kathy McQueen.